FINDING MOTHERHOOD
AN UNEXPECTED JOURNEY

JILL M. MURPHY

Cover Design by Michelle Fairbanks
Edited by Andie Gibson

PRINT ISBN **978-1-5333-9473-6**
Library of Congress Control Number: 2015957025

CONTENTS

"If there's a book you really want to read, but it hasn't been written yet, then you must write it."
—Toni Morrison

I didn't go to school to be a writer. I'm not a well-known author with a shelf full of best sellers. I don't have an extensive vocabulary or use big, fancy words. Writing a book was never something I ever intended to do. What I am is a woman with a beautiful story to share—a story that has allowed me to process feelings of disappointment, loss, heartache, and love. By writing my story down and sharing it, I was able to help my heart heal and find the beauty in my journey to finding motherhood.

This book was written for every pregnant teen, every couple who has experienced infertility, and any family touched by adoption.

I dedicate this book to Joshua, Madeline, and Olivia. You three have made me a mother in different but beautiful ways.

FOREWORD

"My sister and I
My sister and I
Are swinging and swinging
Up to the sky.

Tra-la-la-la
Tra-la-la-lie
This song is called
My sister and I."

From the book *My Sister and I*
Written by Helen E. Buckley

Initially, she wanted to flush me down the toilet, our mom has told us. Forty-four years later she asked me to write the foreword to her book. My first friend, my sister. We did everything together, whether she wanted us to or not. *Charlie's Angels*, Donny and Marie, Danny and Sandy, the playhouse, fake smoking, imaginary boyfriends, make-believe weddings, pregnancies, and seamless childbirth behind the barn; how ironic. We were always playing and practicing for real life, because we knew we would always share real-life moments like these…together.

Then real life was here, and my sister needed me. She was seventeen, pregnant, no one knew, and I suspected. I did the only thing I could do—I told our mom. My sister, the bravest woman I know, began a journey that would change her (and our) life forever.

My sister has experienced both sides of the adoption coin. It has been the most amazing toss-up a person can be a part of.

A few years ago, my sister was having a particularly difficult time navigating the journey and for the millionth time we were talking about it. In a kind of a tongue-and-cheek way I asked her if she googled books on the subject of "so-you-got-pregnant-in-college, gave-the-baby-up-for -adoption, struggled-with-infertility, adopted-2-koreans, and-now-you-are-meeting-your-belly-baby-and-it's-hard-and-you-don't-know-what-to-do?" We laughed.

Then something happened and it went something like this:

In unison, without missing a beat, my sister and I said…"I (You) should write that book."

This is that story.

PREFACE
The Beginning

"There are things about your childhood you hold on to, because they were so much part of you. The places you went, the people you knew."
—The Wonder Years

I ENJOYED A SIMPLE childhood in upstate New York. My family lived in the small town of Chadwicks. It had about 2,500 residents. Nestled in a part of the state where beautiful rolling hills and mature trees gave the landscape a Norman Rockwell feel, it was a town rich with more than one hundred years of history.

Our neighbor was a longtime state senator and a highly respected member of the community, but to us he was simply "Jim." He wore blue coveralls and would help my father and grandfather with yardwork. His daughter was one of our babysitters. One time, Jim caught me kissing a boy behind our garage, and instead of scolding me or telling my parents, he just chuckled and promised to keep my secret. It was just that kind of community.

We spent many days at the park across the street from our house. A small creek ran through it. This was where my father's little brother drowned many years before—a tragic piece of the town's history. There was always one rule before we would leave to play there: "Don't go near the crick!" It wasn't very deep, and I felt invincible, as children generally do. My sister and I would sit on a large, flat rock that was half in the water and look for frogs and fish. We were always safe, but there was a certain feeling of rebellion and triumph in doing it. It was a bit of a miracle that we didn't get caught, considering my father and Jim were the unofficial park security. They would patrol the area at night to keep the park safe and break up any commotion the unruly high school kids created.

We walked to and from school each day. Our school had 250 kids in kindergarten through grade twelve. It was the same school my grandmother and father graduated from. I even had two of the same teachers my father had. My parents were friends with some of the teachers and staff. We didn't dare get in trouble because we knew our parents would find out. (The price we paid for living in a small town.) The positive side of it was we all knew one another and there was never a sense of being alone. There was always someone who knew you and would say hello to you. If you tried out for a sports team or cheerleading, you were pretty much guaranteed a spot because there were so few students!

In the afternoons, we would run around the streets with our friends, from one yard to the next, while our parents and neighbors sat on their front porches visiting over hot coffee or cold beer. When the day was done, Mom would yell out the door, "Girls, time for dinner," and we would come running.

Neighbors were always ready to lend a hand and watch out for one another. When you went to the grocery store or post office you knew everyone you ran into. Just this fact alone encouraged us to keep our noses clean, so to speak.

You simply couldn't get away with much in a community where everyone knew everyone.

My parents, grandparents, relatives, and family friends all had the same basic family structure: the all-American family with two happily married parents and two to three kids. No one was divorced. I lived with my mom, dad, sister Holly, and brother Robert. I am the oldest, with two and a half years between me and my sister, and eight years between me and my brother. We still refer to him as the baby of the family.

That was our model of what life would look like when we were adults. We would graduate, go to college, get married, and have two to three children of our own. That was the plan. It was clean and simple.

My family lived in a beautiful Victorian home that was built in 1901. Like most homes built at that time, it was full of charm and had so many great architectural details. There was beautiful, thick wood trim around all the doorways and windows. It had a wraparound front porch and embellishments on the exterior that always reminded me of a gingerbread house. There were two staircases leading to the second floor—the main stairs in the front and one in the back. A clothesline ran on a pulley going from the back porch out to the barn. The image of my mother hanging out the clothes on that line lives in my memory even all these years later.

My father had grown up in that house, too. I recall my mother and her best friend, Connie, visiting and laughing in the shade of the large gingko and pine trees in front of the house while my siblings and I played on hot summer days. I imagine similar scenes had taken place in the yard decades before when my father was a young boy.

The backyard was lined with lilacs and peonies. My dad had a vegetable garden and my mom had a flower garden.

My siblings and I helped fill them with seedlings in the spring. The old barn behind our house, which we used as a garage, was just as large as our home. It had three stalls up front to park cars in and a lot of space behind that was used for various things such as storing bikes, the lawn mower, and yard tools. But best of all, inside that old barn, was our playhouse.

It was the same playhouse my aunt Peggie played in as a young girl. It had an oriental rug, a twin bed, a play kitchen, dolls, and my mom's old prom dresses, which we used for dress-up. It was magical. Every spring my mom, Holly, and I would open up the large red barn doors, pull all the toys and furniture out onto the grass, and clean it out. Then the summer fun would begin.

The neighbor girls—Lisa, Suzanne, and Maria—and our other friends would come over and we would dress up, fight over the dolls, and play house until we were called in for dinner. Our glider swing by the hollyhocks served as our church pews and our car. We paraded up and down the sidewalk with our dresses and babies. We loved when cars drove by, honked their horns, and waved. As I think back on us, tromping around in too-big taffeta and satin dresses, we must have looked pretty silly, but in our minds we were at the peak of fashion.

Our lives in the playhouse were just as simple and planned as we thought they would be once we were grown up. We would pick full-bloom lilacs for our bridal bouquets and walk down an imaginary aisle between my mom's flower garden and my father's vegetable garden. Our weddings were perfect. Our husbands were usually the invisible Shaun Cassidy, Leif Garrett, or the older boys we always thought were cute in the high school.

When it came time to have our babies, we would stuff a doll under our shirt, go behind the barn, and come back with a baby in our arms. It was that simple. One doll had a hard plastic head and limbs, with a soft body that made her pigeon-toed. We lovingly called her "Chicken Legs." My sister and I still laugh about how we always fought over who got her. I never imagined that my world would be anything less than the magical, structured one we created in that playhouse.

CHAPTER ONE
Plans Change

*"We must be willing to let go of the life we have planned,
so as to have the life that is waiting for us."*
—Joseph Campbell

PART OF THE PLAN I HAD for my life was growing up in that old Victorian house on Elm Street. It was there that I imagined so many of my dreams: going to prom and having pictures taken out back by the lilacs, graduation parties in the barn, sitting on the front porch with my parents planning a wedding. I would one day bring my children to visit their grandparents in the same home where I had visited my grandparents. I envisioned taking my kids to the park across the street to play, just as my mom had done when I was young. I thought one day I might even live in that beautiful old house that was filled with so many memories created by three generations of our family.

Our dining room table truly was the center of our old Victorian home. It was where meals were served, decisions were made, and conversations took place. It was more than a place for my mom to have coffee with her friends or for us to celebrate birthdays and holidays. It was where my sister and I were told the news that we were going to have a baby brother or sister. Years later, it was the place my mom had "the talk" about where babies came from. I would sit at that table to have consequences delivered and be properly lectured about my bad choices.

When I was fifteen, we sat around the dining room table for dinner, like we did every night as a family. But this time, the dinner conversation would be life changing. The company my dad worked for wanted him to work from its headquarters in Minnesota. I sat there quietly, with a mouthful of food, not quite sure how to feel. I didn't know if I was mad at my father for making us leave the world we were so comfortable in, a little excited by the prospect of a new adventure, happy for my dad that he was being offered a new opportunity at work, or sad at the thought of leaving behind my friends and the home I loved. I suppose I felt all of these things in one massive, tornadic swirl of emotions.

In April of my tenth-grade year, we moved to Minnesota. The day we left New York, all our close family friends went to the airport with us and wished us well. We waved good-bye to the life we had in small-town USA, and moved to a suburb of the Twin Cities. I went from a class of thirty-five to a class of almost six hundred. When I told people I had moved from New York, they would be so excited. Of course they thought I had moved from New York *City*—not a small, close-knit town in rural upstate New York. One of my new classmates asked me on the first day of school if I could break-dance. I guess you could say I had reverse culture shock.

I didn't mind the move. I adjusted well and loved our new surroundings. It was weird not to know everyone at the grocery store or in town. But we made friends, got to know the neighbors, and made a new life. We would make the trip back to New York in the summers to visit grandparents, relatives, and friends. We would drive by the old house and feel sad, missing our former home.

The truth is, that was home, and even after living in Minnesota for thirty years, I still feel like that is home for me. When my grandparents died, we had the funeral procession drive slowly down Elm Street and past that big old house. It was such a huge part of our lives.

Our new life in Minnesota was exciting and fun. I met a boy the first week at my new school. We started dating and continued to date into our senior year. He was my first real love. He drove an old VW van, which I thought was so cool. It was the first time I had dated a guy who could drive. The first time I asked if I could go to his house, my mom asked how I would get there. I replied, "He has a van and can drive." Looking back, I'm sure it was one of those moments for my mother when she probably had to let go a little and freak out at the same time. I was no longer a little girl. I was a sophomore in high school, and that came with all sorts of new challenges and beginnings.

It was my first time for many things, including sex. I look back now and think how lucky I was to never get pregnant and how stupid I was to be sexually active at such a young age. Our grand love story ended when his family moved to Texas.

It was time to make new dreams and plans for the future. Although the boy in my image of what my wonderful life would be had changed, the overall picture remained the same. My plan was simple. I would go to college, get a job, meet a wonderful man, get married, have a couple of kids, and live happily ever after. I truly believe God looks at the plans we have for ourselves and chuckles. He had a different plan for me.

CHAPTER TWO
Unexpected Pregnancy

"If we share our story with someone who responds with empathy and understanding, shame cannot survive."
—Brené Brown

THE SUMMER AFTER I graduated from high school was filled with good times and friends. I had been accepted into a state university and was excited for the next chapter in my life. But first, I had a carefree summer of fun to enjoy. I spent my days lying in the sun and my evenings working at a local fast food restaurant and hanging out with friends, doing all the things a typical American teenager does before she goes away to college.

I spent a lot of time hanging out with a guy friend I worked with, Pat, whom I thought I liked as more than a friend. We eventually started dating, and spent many weekend evenings at his house with a group of our friends relaxing, drinking wine coolers, and just having a good time—nothing wild and crazy. One night, we took our dating a little further and had sex. I can still picture the room, feel the heat of the summer, and hear the sound of our friends laughing and talking outside. Then he said the words that will remain etched in my mind forever: "The condom broke."

At first, I couldn't believe it. What were the chances of that happening? Here I thought we were being responsible. I tried to calm my worry by telling myself it was only one time. The chances of me getting pregnant were slim.

While my friends were spending their last few weeks of summer being carefree and looking forward to their new path in life as young adults, I carried an unspoken burden: the nagging unknowing and anxiety of wondering if I might be pregnant.

A month passed, and my parents helped me move to Mankato to start college. Soon I was settled into my dorm and they were on their way. All the while, they had no idea of the worry I had hidden in my heart.

Well into my first semester of college it was confirmed — I was indeed pregnant. I was shocked and so worried. I only shared this life-changing news with Pat and a few of my closest friends. The truth was, I kept myself so busy with my new surroundings and the hustle of life as a college student, attending classes and living on my own, that I was often able to put the fact that I was pregnant out of my mind.

Even as I participated in the normal college routine with my new friends—going to classes and parties, hanging out in our dorm rooms talking—the reality lingered, buried beneath my busyness. I suppose there was a part of me that thought, *If I don't allow myself to think about it, maybe it won't be true*. I tried to keep my mind off what was really worrying me. However, the old saying "out of sight, out of mind" doesn't work very well when your body starts changing.

Pat and I had broken up. I felt as though we were better friends than anything more. We kept in touch very little, but occasionally exchanged letters. There was an added sense of loneliness in feeling like I was traveling this completely unknown path by myself, without a partner in the baby's father, without the support of my family or most of my friends, if only because they had no idea. However, that sense of isolation would soon change.

I went home in March over spring break, and still no one really knew. I suppose the fact that I weighed in at around one hundred pounds and baggy clothes were in style, made it much easier for me to hide my expanding waistline. One afternoon while I was home, I got into a terrible fight with my sister. I don't even remember what it was about, but I'm certain it was over something trivial. I blew up, stormed out of the house, and went for a drive.

Holly had her suspicions about my condition. She took them to our mom and mentioned that she thought I might be pregnant. She pointed out that typically when I gain weight, it settles in my hips and butt (I have my grandma to thank for those genes), and she noticed I had put on weight in my stomach. She also reasoned that I was bitchier to her than normal, which she attributed to the hormonal changes of a pregnant woman and the stress of hiding it.

I returned from my drive to find my mom cleaning the house. When my mother cleans, the walls could cave in around her and she wouldn't deviate from her cleaning until it was done. This time, she immediately dropped the vacuum cleaner and rushed upstairs to her sewing room. She hollered down for me to come up because she had bought some new patterns for Capri pants, and she wanted to measure me.

Normally, I loved it when my mom made new clothes for me. She was a great seamstress and this was an era when homemade clothes were actually considered cool. But instead of excitement at the prospect of new clothes, I was horrified. As I walked up the steps, I convinced myself that there was nothing to worry about. I would just suck my stomach in. Unfortunately, that doesn't really work very well when you're six months pregnant.

"You've put a little weight on," my mother said.

"Oh, you know—freshman fifteen," I responded with a nervous chuckle.

Then it happened; the moment I had been trying to avoid since I realized I was pregnant. She looked into my eyes, and with all seriousness asked, "Jill, are you pregnant?"

I wanted to lie. I even tried to deny it, but then I let it all out and told her the truth. I felt awful that I had kept such a huge secret from my family, but I told her I wanted to figure out my plans before I shared the news with anyone.

My mother immediately got out the phone book and called Planned Parenthood to see what resources they might have. I knew I wanted to place my baby up for adoption and Pat had agreed with me. I was eighteen and just beginning to figure out how to take care of myself. How could I possibly be a good mother?

My mom hugged me and assured me it would all be all right. Looking back, I can't believe I actually thought my parents would be anything but supportive. I'm sure they were disappointed, but they hid any sign of it. They gave me nothing but their unconditional love.

In the months to come, I spent the remainder of my freshman year of college going to classes, seeing my counselor at Catholic Charities, looking at profiles of eager parents waiting for a baby to complete their families, and attending appointments. I will never forget my first OB/GYN appointment or the crabby, older doctor. His first comment to me—a scared, pregnant teen—was, "You sure waited long enough to see a doctor."

His words felt like a slap across my face. Obviously, I already felt guilty for waiting so long, for living the past six months of my life trapped inside a lie. But young naïveté and denial can be powerful things. I wanted to say, "Yes, thank you for noticing, jerk!" I hoped he wouldn't be the one who would deliver my baby.

I ended up seeing all the doctors at the clinic to ensure that when it was time for me to give birth, all the doctors would know my "circumstance" and I would be sure to see a familiar face at the delivery. I had a favorite doctor at the clinic. He was kind and empathetic to my situation. He also had two adopted sons of his own. He understood and never made me feel like a lesser person for my situation.

While most people spent spring quarter lying in the sun, going to parties, and making plans for the summer, I was planning for and thinking about the type of life this baby growing inside of me would have—not with me, but with that perfect family I picked out. It wasn't the typical first year of college most kids my age experienced. I spent so much time planning and picturing my child's future. I assumed Pat had similar thoughts. Surely he would also want what was best, and in my mind, adoption was the only good option.

Being a pregnant teen was a struggle. I learned quickly who was truly there to support me. I realized which of my "friends" were more interested in gossiping about my situation than helping me through it.

As my freshman year came to an end, I still had a few weeks until my due date. My counselor from Catholic Charities, Gloria, welcomed me into her home and treated me like part of her family. With only two weeks until delivery, it made more sense to stay in Mankato where my doctors were than to go back to my parents' house.

One evening I was having funny pains in my lower back. I wasn't quite sure what was causing them, so I mentioned it to Gloria. She told me she thought I was going into labor. I'm so grateful I had her with me because I'm not sure I would have recognized them as labor pains. It wasn't how I expected to feel.

I called my parents, then Gloria took me to the hospital. It all went so fast. The baby was breech so I ended up having a C-section. Of course, the doctor on call that night was the crabby one who I'd hoped would *not* be the one to deliver my baby. All the doctors and staff knew my situation. They put a sheet up between me and my belly so I wouldn't see anything. I chose not to see the baby because I feared it would be way too hard on me emotionally to see him, knowing I would have to let him go.

On June 16, I gave birth to a healthy baby boy who weighed in at seven pounds, seven ounces. By the time I got out of surgery, my parents had arrived and were waiting for me. It's funny that I was legally an adult, a woman who had just had a baby, since I was so excited and relieved to see my "mommy and daddy."

The next morning, the empathetic doctor with two adopted sons of his own stopped in to visit me. That single action stands out in my mind as one of the kindest gestures in my life. In the midst of my heartache and shame, that doctor made me feel like I was okay. I was more than a number in the record-keeping statistics of teen pregnancy. I mattered.

In the days that followed, I signed papers to relinquish my parental rights. The documents stipulated that the birth father and I would have ten business days to change our minds. The time between the birth and the signing of those papers seemed to rush past, and I felt like I really didn't have time to "feel" the emotions of it all.

This baby boy, whom I had carried in my womb for nine months, would soon be on the way to his new family where he would be loved and cared for and have the life I planned and dreamed of for him. Knowing he would be in a good home with two loving parents made my heart feel full. It was a fullness that would have to cover up the sadness and grief I felt over the loss of my baby. Although I had tried to put him "out of sight, out of mind" for so many months, I had grown to love and cherish him in a way I didn't even know was possible.

I clung to the peace of knowing my baby would be loved by his adoptive parents, and I knew I would live my life loving him too, even if I never saw him. I hoped, in some way, the pain I endured in letting him go would ensure him the life I knew I couldn't give him at the time. The moments were mostly bitter, being so filled with sadness, but I tried to focus on the sweetness of my baby's future.

CHAPTER THREE
Change of Heart

"Resilience is accepting your new reality, even if it's less good than before. You can fight it, you can do nothing but scream about what you've lost, or you can accept that and try to put together something that's good."
—Elizabeth Edwards

AFTER I WAS RELEASED from the hospital, my parents drove me home. The baby would soon be with his wonderful family. Just a month earlier, I sat in my counselor Gloria's office at Catholic Charities reading through the biographies of couples who wanted so desperately to adopt a child. The pair I selected for him seemed perfect.

I slowly started to fold up all the feelings I had—loss, sadness, and grief—and packed them away nicely into a place I couldn't bear to go to. I found myself wondering, "Now what? How do I go on?" But I knew I needed to focus on the future. I had to allow myself to start the summer and trust that my baby boy would have a wonderful life and would someday be able to understand my choice. I needed to believe that one day he would understand that I loved him enough to put his needs before any wants I had. He was more important.

I sat on the couch still recovering from my C-section—a scar that will always remind me of that difficult time—when the baby's father came to my parents' house. I thought it was nice of him to stop by to check on me and see how I was doing since we hadn't spoken in quite a few months. It didn't take him long to get to the reason behind his visit.

He said, "I want to talk about our son."

When he said the words "our son," it caught me off guard. He was no longer "ours," and in a sense never really was. *We* had chosen adoption, to let another mother and father call him by that title. *We* had decided it was the best decision because we were so young.

I said, "He isn't our son. I accidentally got pregnant, and now he will be with *his* family; the family I picked out."

His reply shocked me to my core. He said, "I have a lawyer, and I am taking you to court for custody."

I don't even remember what I said next. I stood frozen in a spinning room. After he left, I went to tell my mom what had just happened. It rocked my world. I was beyond devastated and hurt. My parents were furious. The perfect plan we had made for this tiny, sweet baby was being disrupted and changed. In my mind, I screamed, "No! No! No! This is not what I pictured and planned for him!" I wanted him to have two mature and loving parents who could give him the world, not a single parent who was barely out of high school. I wanted my baby to have a stable home, a white picket fence—the whole American Dream. I wanted him to grow up happy and healthy with no doubt he was loved.

My parents decided to get a lawyer and fight for this baby's future. We went to the yellow pages and found a female attorney who practiced family law. I thought how a woman lawyer would be nice; maybe she could empathize with my decision. She told us she couldn't take the case because it would be a conflict of interest. She had already been retained as *his* lawyer.

We decided to find a lawyer based in Mankato where the baby had been born. Many phone calls, meetings, and lots of money later, we lost. The court basically said if the mother *didn't want* the baby, custody would go to the father.

I thought, "Didn't want? You have got to be kidding me!" It was never a matter of wanting my baby or not. I wanted him, but more than what I perceived as my own selfish desires, I wanted what was *best* for him. I felt as if the court treated my sweet, innocent baby like a car or a piece of property. They failed to recognize that he was the product of two young people who were incapable of being parents.

I wasn't sure how I could go on from that. It was hard. I was furious that my wonderfully planned life for this baby had been turned upside down and sideways. The worst part was, there was nothing I could do about it.

I had a whole new list of worries. I was so afraid that I might run into my baby's dad and the baby would be with him. We only lived a town apart. How would I react if I saw my baby? Would feelings surface that I wouldn't be able to deal with?

I slowly came to terms with the new situation. There was nothing I could do but accept it. I hoped and prayed his father knew what he was doing and would love him and give him what he needed unconditionally. Although it wasn't ideal for such a young man to become a single father, at least I knew Pat was a good guy and came from a wonderful family who would support him.

About a year later, Pat got married. His wife wanted to legally adopt my baby. I signed the papers saying it was okay. I found comfort in knowing that now he would have a mother. Although my heart was warmed by the knowledge that he would have two parents, I still worried. I struggled to feel confident that this was all truly best for him.

One day, around Christmastime, my dad and I were at Kmart, and from a distance I saw Pat across the store with a little, blond-haired boy in a cart. It was the moment I had dreaded with a fear that had eaten at my soul and kept me up at night. It was him. They were heading to the checkout. I ducked in an aisle and hid. I was nervous, scared, and curious. I felt faint. My heart threatened to beat through my chest.

When my dad found me, all the color had drained from my face. He could see that something was wrong. I told him who I had seen. He asked if I wanted to leave. We chose to stay and finish our shopping, but I will never forget the way I felt or the thought I had when I saw him. He looked so much like my brother at that age.

I try to look back on that time without allowing regret to creep in. I can't regret that I wanted more for my baby and thought adoption was the best choice. I *do* regret not having communication with his father during my pregnancy. We could have had conversations. Maybe I wouldn't have been so blindsided that day when he showed up at my parents' home. Maybe, if we had talked, *my* plan could have been *our* plan; two young adults working together on a decision that was right for this baby boy.

Looking back, I wonder how his new wife felt. She was marrying a young man with a baby. She was vested in this little boy; had grown to love him as any mother loves her child. She loved him enough to adopt him, and she was given the right of motherhood by law, and, because of the love in her heart, the gift for him to call her "Mom." She would share all his "firsts." *She* was the lucky one. Did she ever worry that I might show up at any moment wanting to be part of his life? I wondered if she felt slighted by marrying someone who already had a child at such a young age. I still wonder those things sometimes, but I am confident she opened her heart fully and completely to love that baby. *She* was his mother.

I can look back now and know that the decision I made was the right one for me, and in my heart, I was making the choice I thought was best for my child. I accepted the court's decision and made peace with it. I kept my feelings folded up and tucked away. It probably wasn't the healthiest thing to do. Sometimes I wonder how on earth I made it through that time without losing my mind, and how I found the strength to trust my decision at such a young and immature age.

Going through that made me grow up fast in so many ways. At the time, I couldn't begin to understand how this one year of my life would become an important piece to a bigger puzzle that God had created for me. It was the beginning of a complicated journey — my journey to motherhood.

CHAPTER FOUR
Finding Love

"Love is patient, love is kind. It does not envy, it does not boast, it is not proud. It is not rude, it is not self-seeking, it is not easily angered, it keeps no record of wrongs. Love does not delight in evil, but rejoices with the truth. It always protects, always trusts, always hopes, always perseveres. Love never fails. But where there are prophecies they will cease; where there are tongues, they will be stilled; where there is knowledge, it will pass away. For we know in part and we prophesy in part, but when perfection comes, the imperfect disappears. When I was a child, I talked like a child, I thought like a child, I reasoned like a child. When I became a man, I put the childish ways behind me. Now we see but a poor reflection as in a mirror; then we shall see face to face. Now I know in part; then I shall know fully, even as I am fully known. And now these three remain: faith, hope, and love. But the greatest of these is love."
—1 Corinthians 13:4–13

I NEVER FINISHED COLLEGE. I studied psychology for about three years before I decided reading books and writing papers wasn't for me. I had a creative streak and was very right-brained, but I had no idea what to do with it.

I was working two jobs—one at a flower shop, and the other as a manager for the craft department at Walmart. Although I didn't love retail, both jobs allowed me to use a bit of my creative side. I was twenty-four and shared an apartment with my friend Amy, who also worked at the flower shop. It was a fun time in life. Many of my friends were getting engaged and married, and moving away. Two of my really good friends were getting married that fall and I was in both of their weddings.

Although it was a happy time and I was thrilled for my friends, I was in a different place personally. I had recently broken up with my boyfriend of two years. My happily ever after was nowhere in sight. It was time to cut my losses and move on.

In September of 1992, I was the maid of honor in a friend's wedding. I was rocking my green satin dress, matching dyed shoes, and permed '90s hairdo. The day was filled with beautiful flowers and laughter. The reception was a wonderful celebration with a great band, and the wedding party danced all night.

Another girl who was also in the wedding party decided we should do "the alligator." For those unfamiliar with this dance move (and I use that term loosely), the alligator involves lying on your back and wiggling your arms and legs up in the air. When you've had a couple of drinks, you really believe it will be funny. We did it, and we thought we were quite hilarious, although I'm sure there were others who just found the sight ridiculous.

Occasionally, I went up to the guitar player in the band to request songs. He was cute and friendly, and I immediately felt a connection. When the band was done playing and the night was winding down, the guitar player introduced himself as Mike and chatted with me for a few minutes.

There was something about him. When he talked to me he looked into my eyes and I felt a sense of warmth. I felt as though I had known him more than just an evening's worth of song requests. The wedding party was getting ready to head out, and the band was starting to pack up. I felt a sense of panic as I wondered, *"What if I never see this guy again?"* I worked up enough courage to give him my phone number.

The next day, Mike called. I'm sure it was my great dance moves, especially my expertly executed alligator, that sealed the deal for him. I was excited and nervous all at the same time.

He asked, "So are you married, or what?"

I laughed and replied, "No. Are you?"

He was divorced. Naturally, I was curious about his age. I mean, he had already been married and divorced. He told me he was thirty-one, an *older guy with a real job*. So different than the other guys I had dated. We made small talk. I explained I had just broken up with a guy, and I kind of blew him off. He was polite about it and left me his number in case I changed my mind.

A good month went by before Mike called again.

He said, "I don't know if you remember me. I was the band guy from the wedding."

Of course I remembered him! He asked me out, and this time I said yes. A week later we went to dinner and listened to a band. He was so easy to talk to that we chatted the whole night. I sat on his lap, telling him about my family, my life, and also being a pregnant teen. He was understanding and could relate in a way because his younger sister had gone through a similar situation. I felt comfort in that. It was a little bit of a connection to him that came through something painful I had experienced.

From that night forward, Mike and I saw each other regularly. He would leave notes in my car, bring me lunch, and I found myself missing him on the days I couldn't see him. After several months had passed, he surprised me with a sweet gesture. I had spent the night at his place. He woke me up in the morning before he left for work, and said, "I put my key on your key chain. Have a good day." Then he kissed me good-bye.

I was head over heels! He was romantic, funny, sweet, and kind. I couldn't imagine ever being without him.

The first Christmas after we started dating, I invited Mike to meet my family and spend Christmas day with us. He brought a bottle of wine with a ribbon on it for my parents. (He told me later he had gone over to his boss's house, and she told him he couldn't go empty-handed so she set him up with the wine.) I was thrilled to see my parents and siblings hit it off with him. There was an easiness about how he related to my family. It was as if he belonged.

It was time to meet Mike's family. The day I was going to meet his mom, maternal grandparents, and his sister, Liz, was exciting, but naturally, I was also a bit nervous. When we were a block from his mom's house, he gave me a strange look.

"What?" I asked anxiously.

Mike replied, "I just hope you make a good impression."

I slapped his arm, and we both laughed. Luckily, the day went smoothly, and I felt at ease with his family.

Soon after, I got to meet his grandma Veronica on his dad's side. She asked how we met. Mike told her we met at a wedding, and I gave him my number.

His grandma replied, "Oh, she's a hussy, is she?"

My heart jumped into my throat for a second before I realized she was kidding. Then we all laughed. Mike and I still laugh about that today.

In the spring of 1993 he asked me to move in with him. I was thrilled. We lived in a little one-bedroom apartment. At one time, the space had been used as an old milking house and was later converted into two apartments. We combined our belongings, settled in, and named it the "Love Shack." With ugly gold carpet, fuzzy velvet wallpaper on one wall in the kitchen, and water that was so hard it made our clothes feel like sandpaper, it was our home. We slept on a hide-a-bed couch.

As humble as it was, it was the start to a wonderful new beginning, a place where we would make many wonderful memories.

That fall, a year after we had been dating, we went away for the weekend. As we were getting ready to go out to dinner, Mike announced he had a gift for me. Modestly wrapped inside a sheet of newspaper, I found a magazine. I turned it over, trying to figure out what was going on. It was *Brides* magazine. The next thing I knew, he had a ring in his hand and was asking me to marry him. I was shocked and beyond happy. Of course I would marry him.

The year that followed found us busy planning our wedding and house hunting. It was time to give up the $250-a-month "Love Shack" and buy our first real home. In April of 1994 we made that piece of our American dream come true. It was so exciting to be unpacking, painting, and planning our future together. We discussed things like which room would someday become a baby nursery, what kind of table we wanted to buy to replace the Nordic Track we had in the center of our dining room, and whether or not we should rebuild the deck. There were so many things in life to look forward to inside the walls of our first home.

In September, we were married. It was a wonderful day of celebration. All our family and friends traveled from near and far to help us make the day magical and perfect. One of the biblical readings we chose was from 1 Corinthians chapter 13, verses 4 through 8. Chances are you've heard this one before. It begins with "Love is patient, love is kind." Little did we know that patience was going to be the key to starting the family we dreamed of having together.

CHAPTER FIVE
Wanting Children

"Sometimes you're not given what you want because something better is planned for you instead."
—Unknown

MIKE AND I WERE MARRIED and excited about our future. All our hopes and dreams were ahead of us, especially the dream of being parents. We were happy, in love, and had our first home. Life was beginning to look much like the imaginary world my friends and I had created in the playhouse so many years before.

A year into our marriage, Mike and I decided it was time to start a family, so I went off birth control. We didn't consciously try—we just went on with our lives. At the same time, many of our friends around us were trying to get pregnant as well. We never imagined our trying would literally include blood, sweat, and tears.

For six to eight months, we tried to casually let nature take its course. Each month, I found myself not pregnant. We began to wonder, *"What gives?"* In the back of my mind I thought about when I was seventeen and how easily I had gotten pregnant accidentally one summer night. Now, when I was ready and eagerly waiting for it to happen, it seemed to be taking forever.

At the time, I was seeing the same doctor who had delivered my baby eight years before. He was a wonderful doctor, but he tended to be of the "old-school persuasion." (Dare I say, he was a bit of a crotchety old man.) When I told him we had been trying and nothing was happening, he gave me some really profound advice.

"Relax. Light some candles. It will happen."

Outwardly, I shrugged that perhaps he could be right. But inside I screamed, "Gee, thanks. That thought *never* crossed my mind. Isn't that what newlyweds are doing anyway?"

We decided it was time to move on to an infertility specialist. She thought the doctor's advice to us was ridiculous and agreed we needed to get to the bottom of what was happening, or not happening, as the case seemed to be. The next few years were filled with all kinds of fun. When I say fun, I mean doctor visits, testing, giving samples of unmentionable bodily fluids, poking and prodding, and lab technician–supervised bloodletting.

First we started with Mike. His test was simple enough. They needed to see if his "boys could swim." After an awkward office visit and the walk of shame back to a private room, we learned that his boys could swim with the best of them. With confirmation that his sperm could qualify for the Olympic team, Mike stood a little taller and walked a little straighter. It was as if he had won the gold medal of sperm count.

The boost in masculine pride presented us with some much-welcomed humor. He'd strut into the room a bit like George Clooney high off the news of being selected again as the world's sexiest man, and I could only shake my head, smile, and say, "Yes, Mike, you're the man." But as I patted him on the back for his ability to produce sperm that could swim upstream in a hurricane and still have energy to implant themselves into an egg, the realization began to sink in. If it wasn't something wrong with him, it was something wrong with me. So the focus shifted in my direction.

I started taking my temperature every morning and charting it to see when I would ovulate. Then we had a twenty-four-hour window, and no matter how inconvenient, we had to make it work. The song "Afternoon Delight" played in my mind as we rushed home over lunch for a quick attempt at baby-making. The term "nooner" had become literal.

When this plan of attack didn't produce results, we went further. When I ovulated I had to go into the clinic and get a hormone shot in my hip *that* day. That meant going in late to work or leaving early to make sure I got it done within the all-important twenty-four-hour window. Getting a shot was bad enough, but the side effects were even worse. It gave me terrible adnominal cramps, which made me super uncomfortable and grumpy. This was not a recipe for romance. It had all become so scientific.

Months turned into years. I would grasp at any hint that I might be pregnant. If I gagged slightly while brushing my teeth, I thought, "I must be nauseous." Which led to the next thought, "I might be pregnant." Which sent me rushing to the nearest drugstore to purchase twenty dollars' worth of pregnancy tests, all of which were negative. *Again.* I kept convincing myself that I could be pregnant, and *this* was finally the time it had worked, but it hadn't. And my heart broke all over again, month after month.

The giggling stopped. Being intimate had become a *chore*, and still we were no closer to having a baby. We were burned out and decided to take a bit of a break from doctors.

In the next year, Mike switched jobs, and we moved from Mankato up to the Twin Cities. It was an exciting time.

We both had great jobs, our new home was bigger, and we were closer to my family.

We were ready to start the process again. We found a new doctor who was awesome. He basically asked, "How aggressive do you want to be?"

I underwent a laparoscopy, which involved having dye shot through my fallopian tubes as the doctors went in through my belly button with a scope to thoroughly look for any type of scarring. If they found any scar tissue, they would try to remove it. It was painful—physically and emotionally.

When the procedure was over, I was sitting in the hospital bed, drowsy and in pain, when Mike told me the doctors had news. Then my doctor came in and showed me pictures of my fallopian tubes. They were scarred so badly that they were completely shut.

The only way we could conceive a child was to have my tubes removed and try in vitro fertilization. That meant more doctors, surgery, and disappointment. I was done. I couldn't take any more.

We went home and, exhausted from the procedure and from hearing the results, I slept. When I woke up, my mom was there. She and Mike had been talking about our situation. The news really hadn't hit me until then. It was *my* fault. We couldn't have a child because of *me*. *I* could not get pregnant. The realization hit me and I cried.

My mom said, "This is not how it's supposed to happen."

For the first time in my life, I questioned my faith. I wondered why God would allow this. Was He punishing me for the decision I made years earlier to not keep the baby He had given me then? Mike and I both spent a lot of time being angry, hurt, and longing so badly for a baby. We grieved for the loss of the dream we had. The image I had created in my mind of the perfect family was beginning to blur.

The irony was like a hard slap from an iron fist. At a time when I couldn't be the best mom, I became pregnant. When I was ready to be a great mom—nothing. Nothing but sadness and heartbreak. I felt like a failure.

The feeling of loss took a toll on Mike and me, individually and as a couple. Even after we knew having a child was no longer an option for us, the desire was still strong.

Many people tried to be helpful by giving advice.

"Oh, just don't think about it, and it will happen."

"Once you relax it will happen."

"It will happen when it's meant to be."

Their well-intentioned words made me feel trapped inside the center of a tornado. The flurry of thoughts and advice left me spinning. Some days, I wanted to crawl inside myself and hide.

Then there were a few people who would ask, "Will you go find your birth son now?"

Of course I wouldn't. None of this was about him. This was about Mike and me, and the painful reality that we would never be able to have children. I found myself wondering if they really thought I would say, "Oh . . . great idea! I can't have a child with my husband, but I did have one when I was a teenager. I think I'll go find him, and he'll take the place of the child Mike and I were hoping for."

Maybe there was a certain sort of twisted logic in their question, but I always wondered how anyone could ask such a thing. My birth son's needs always went before my wants. I would never disrupt a young boy's happy and settled life because of something I couldn't have.

I was at the point in my life when all my friends were getting pregnant. It felt like everywhere I turned, there was a blossoming baby bump in my path and another baby shower to attend. I would paste on a fake smile and say with as much enthusiasm as possible, "Oh, that's great news." As the words came out of my mouth, I hoped to God I sounded sincere. It wasn't that I didn't want my friends and family to be happy and have families, but inside, I just wanted to scream and cry, "It's not fair!"

We decided after almost six years of riding the infertility roller coaster to close the door on all the doctors, medical jargon, and forced intimacy. The one thing we knew for sure was that we desperately wanted a child, and we had to think about where to go next. It was a major relief to stop trying, stop going to the doctor, stop taking advice from everyone—and to have moments of intimacy because we *wanted* to, not because we *had* to. It was time to just enjoy being a couple again.

CHAPTER SIX
Mourning

"New beginnings are often disguised as painful endings."
—Lao Tzu

WHEN PEOPLE DIE we mourn for them. In some cases we are devastated by their deaths. In other cases we are saddened by the loss but grateful they are no longer suffering. We celebrate their lives with wakes and say good-bye with funerals. We have support from family, friends, and the community. These supporters understand our loss because they have likely dealt with similar losses. Life seems a little emptier when loved ones leave us, but as time passes, the sadness is lessened, and we begin to pick up the pieces and move forward. We still miss them, but soon we are able to smile as we remember all the good times. Their memories warm our hearts, enabling us to resume our normal lives.

But what do you do when a *dream* dies? There's no wake, no funeral, no "Jell-O salad with buttered-bun ham sandwich" luncheon. No proper good-bye. Family, friends, and those around you don't understand—unless they, too, have experienced a similar loss. Although it is a symbolic death, the grieving process is the same as a death in the family—sadness, anger, bargaining, denial, and acceptance.

My husband and I were grieving because our dream died. Our beautiful bubble popped, and the vision of getting pregnant and creating a baby that was a part of us both was shattered before our eyes. It was clinically and very matter-of-factly confirmed by the results of countless tests and procedures.

We muddled through as though we weren't sure what to do next. We had talked so much about our "someday baby." I had the baby room planned in my head and even bought a pair of little baby socks I was going to wrap in a box and give to Mike when I found out I was pregnant. Now those things would never happen.

I screamed and cried out to God, "Why?!" I couldn't shake the thought that He was punishing me for my past actions and the decisions I made as a pregnant teen. I found myself bargaining with God. "If I pray more and go to church more, will you take away this pain?"

Although I did give birth, I was never allowed to experience the fullness, the joy, the completeness of the experience because of timing and circumstances. I had to make the sacrifice. I loved my baby so much, that I chose adoption for him. I had to treat myself as a vessel for a baby to grow and remove emotion from that pregnancy to be able to give my son the wonderful life he deserved.

After all these years, I still mourn that loss. I would never experience the anticipation one feels during those anxious minutes while a pregnancy test processes to show the tiny blue line that changes your whole life. I would never experience the excitement of telling my spouse, "I'm pregnant! We're having a baby!" There would be no big hug and happy tears over a long-awaited pregnancy. We would never experience the happiness of sharing the news with our family and friends. There would be no doctor's appointment to hear our baby's heartbeat for the first time. We would never eagerly watch the screen during an ultrasound to see if we could determine the sex of our baby. My husband would never put his hand on my belly to feel our baby kick for the first time. We would not share in that moment of delivering our baby while he squeezed my hand, encouraging me to breathe. We would never see our beautiful baby for the first time and hear his or her first cry.

I mourned the loss of our DNA coming together to create a person. It took some time for me to accept that we wouldn't have children who looked like us. We would never look at our child and remark how she looks like Aunt Peggie when she was a little girl. Or how much he resembles my dad as a boy. Our child wouldn't have my husband's eyes or the same cowlick I have in my hair. We wouldn't be able to compare our children's pictures to our own pictures at their age. There would be no shared birthmarks, hair color, or allergies.

I mourned all these things. I still have periods of anger about it. I still cry about it now and then and ponder the "what ifs." When my mom shows pictures of my aunt to my sister and tells her how much her daughter looks like her, I am reminded that I don't get to share moments like that. I even remember the look my dad and mom had when they saw my niece for the first time. It was a look of recognition. As if they were looking at one of their own, a baby so similar to the babies they had created together. I had to accept that I would never have that.

No one can understand this kind of loss unless they have experienced it. Sure, people can try to empathize with you, but they still don't *get it*. It's funny how even now, at the age of forty-seven, I still mourn. Some emotions pursue you throughout your life. They take your breath away when you least expect them to. Even when it seems I have resolved the issue within my own heart, it can come back and suddenly hurt again. Sometimes, I can cry out of nowhere over this thing I have no control over.

Such experiences are supposed to make us grow and learn, to appreciate a new path that never crossed our minds before. Yet, it is incredibly difficult for us to imagine anything beyond the scope of how we have planned our entire lives.

I learned to bury these emotions deep in my heart. I feared if I ever let them out for the world to see, there might be no way to stop them. I learned to show the world my smile, silliness, and positive attitude, and I learned to hide away the sadness, frustration, and anger that still simmers deep inside of me.

The void of my old dream would always be there, but I resolved to move on to a *new* dream. I would set my sights on a different vision. The goal of having children was the same, but now there was a different plan. This was the path God had chosen for me, and I was ready to travel it, full speed ahead.

CHAPTER SEVEN
Choosing Adoption

"Sometimes things happen in life that are not part of the plan. When that happens, don't give up on your dreams, just find another way to reach them."
—Ritu Ghatourey

MIKE AND I PUT TO REST the dream of getting pregnant. We did not, however, let go of our dream to become parents. We thought about our choices and decided on adoption. It was roughly the same cost as in vitro fertilization, but we would have a better chance of getting a baby at the end of adoption. It felt so good to put the medical part to rest and focus on our new path. Although we decreased the medical portion of our journey, we definitely upped the paperwork piece by 100 percent!

During the summer and fall of 2000 we dove in. We went through Children's Home Society and got all the information we needed to start the process. The process was tedious and time consuming. When you adopt a child, you need to prove yourself. You need to be able to support a child financially, emotionally, and physically. You need to be in good health, have a loving relationship, and be able to provide a safe and nurturing home.

I found the process rather ironic when I looked around and saw incidences of others who had no right being parents, but seemed to be blessed with an abundance of fertility: the parents who were addicted to drugs or alcohol and had more kids than they could support. The women who kept bringing children into the midst of a marriage riddled with spousal abuse. The couples who abused their children sexually, physically, or mentally, yet kept having more babies. Or the young girl who found herself in the same situation I was as a teen who chose to keep her child but was unable to give him the best life possible. And here sat me and Mike. Before we could adopt, we would be put under a microscope to make sure we were fit to be parents.

When we started the process, there were meetings to attend, countries to research, papers to obtain, and history to sort through. We needed copies of marriages, divorces, birth certificates, income statements—anything and everything that would trace back to us, either favorably or not. We were "normal" people who just wanted to be parents. We both had jobs and a cozy, warm, safe home. We both had families filled with love. The only skeleton in our closets was maybe a speeding ticket or a minor alcohol consumption. If we left anything out that may be important, we would be questioned. It took several months to obtain all the necessary information.

We also needed references. There were so many forms to fill out and get notarized, and there were fees for everything. The cost was high, but then again, how do you put a price on a baby?

A social worker came to see our home and visit with us. Talk about wanting the house to be perfectly spotless! We needed an FBI fingerprint and background check. We had to prove we were ready to be parents and worthy enough for the gift of a baby.

We chose to go through South Korea for our adoption. A baby born out of wedlock there was like a big black X on a family's honor. In their culture, if a young, unmarried woman got pregnant, they always chose adoption. No man would ever want to marry her. No family of any man would want her to marry their son.

As I learned about the taboo of unwed mothers in South Korea, I found it odd. It mirrored how our culture was in the '50s and '60s. Although it's good that teen pregnancy doesn't carry the stigma in our nation that it once did, it's sad to see that teen pregnancy has become more common here.

My parents joined us as we attended a weekend workshop about Korean culture and history, which was presented by the woman who started the Korean Adoption program for Children's Home Society. It was interesting to learn all about the country our child would someday come from. My dad had been stationed in South Korea while he was in the army, which seemed to be a meaningful coincidence.

Somewhere within the mounds of forms and paperwork, we could choose the sex of the baby. We decided on a baby girl. Along with that decision, we were given a checklist. We had to decide what medical scenarios we would or would not accept in a child. The agency and social workers were very good about explaining that it was okay to say no to certain things. Everyone who is expecting a baby wants a happy and healthy child. Why would we wish for anything less?

My mom was a nurse so she could help me make sense of the medical conditions that were listed. The social workers made it clear that there were certain people who could accept issues that we may not be able to, and that was all right. It felt so strange to make such decisions in regard to the human being we were preparing to bring into our family. In a sense, I felt as if we were playing God.

I really think buying a home requires fewer signatures than adopting a baby. We finished our paperwork and sent it in. Then, our form went to the bottom of the pile, and all we could do was wait.

We were told it could be up to six months before we got a referral, which is a call that the agency makes to the expectant parents when they have a baby who meets the specifications outlined by all that paperwork we completed. Then the hopeful parents could look at the picture, scan through the paperwork, and say yes or no. I couldn't imagine saying no!

We both kept busy with work and life and anxiously wondered when that call would come. Then one day, while I was at work, I was paged that I had a call.

I jokingly said to my coworkers, "You never know when it will be *the call*."

It had only been three months of waiting, so I truly never imagined that this would be the phone call that would change my life forever. But sure enough, a baby girl had been born on December 27. It was a moment I can only describe as crazy, exciting, and surreal.

I called Mike right away and said, "We have a baby!" Finally, the child we had been dreaming of was here.

Mike stopped by the agency and picked up our packet—the most important packet we had ever opened. It was filled with all the info about our baby and even included a photo. She was a chubby-cheeked girl with Asian eyes and dark hair. She was beautiful, and she was all ours! Her birth mother had been sixteen. Oh, how I could relate. We signed the papers indicating that we wanted this precious baby, and then we waited some more.

We prepared the room; painted, bought furniture, and got everything ready. It was the middle of March and we thought we had a good six months. My sister and close friend had planned a shower for us for Saturday, May 19. On May 16 we got a phone call from the agency telling us that our baby would be in our arms in just two days.

"Gotcha Day" was Friday, May 18, 2001. Our entire family waited at the airport gate, as you could do in those days before 9/11, watching with great anticipation as everyone got off the plane. We strained to get our first glance at the newest member of our family. After what seemed like an eternity, we finally saw our baby, riding in a Korean sling around her Korean escort's neck. She was all smiles and chubby cheeks. Although she wasn't quite five months old, and we'd only known about her for a short time, we had waited a lifetime for her. Her Korean name was Jeong Ah Lee. We would name her Madeline Elizabeth Lee Murphy and call her Maddie.

We started her first day off with us right—with a baby shower. She was admired and doted on by our family and friends while she slept most of the time. She was given everything a baby could need or want. In return, she gave me all I had been hoping for. She made me a mommy. I loved her instantly and completely.

Her first week with us required Mike and me to do a lot of tag-team walking and bouncing while our baby adjusted to the fifteen-hour time change and recovered from jet lag. It was a beautiful, wonderful time.

God had given us the baby we had always wanted. I felt as though my faith in Him had been restored. Maybe, just maybe, His plan for us was even better than the one we had envisioned for ourselves.

CHAPTER EIGHT
Adoption Again

"Stay patient and trust your journey."
—Unknown

WHEN MADDIE WAS NEARLY three, we were blessed with a nice tax return. I know, you are wondering what the two have to do with anything. The fact is, we had been discussing that we wanted another child and that Maddie needed a sibling. Since we had been blessed with a little extra money, we decided to go through the process again.

Mike and I discussed whether we should select a boy or girl this time. Neither one of us really had an opinion on the gender we chose. Since we already had all the things a girl would need, we figured, why not get Maddie a sister. I loved having both a sister and a brother when I was growing up, but Maddie and the new baby would be the same age difference that my sister and I are, so I knew what a special relationship they could have.

We had the same lengthy process to go through as last time; the truckloads of paperwork and the same multitude of fees. At least this time around, we felt more organized about it all. We turned in our paperwork, and waited once again. We got "the call" for baby girl number two in the fall of 2003. Her given name was Jo Ah Park. Once again, we were utterly excited.

Our social worker told us she had been in the hospital for the first week after her birth. Although she was carried to term, she was only four pounds. They told us a lot of big medical words that I didn't understand, but I knew that she had a few seizures and some of her APGAR numbers were low. Mike and I were both worried.

In the stacks of paperwork, we had again completed the medical form indicating what we felt we could accept. I knew they paid very close attention to this when matching babies to families. Still, we needed some reassurance. I called my doctor's office and explained that we needed a doctor to translate the medical jargon and tell us what all the tests and notes meant in plain English.

In fact, we were so nervous and concerned that we waited to tear open the envelope with her photo in it. What if she had a medical condition we didn't feel capable of handling? I couldn't bear to have her beautiful face in my mind until we knew for certain she would be ours.

The doctor we met with was an older gentleman. My history with older male doctors had left me with an opinion of them that wasn't very high. But this doctor was wonderful. He was kind, gentle, and so understanding.

He looked through all the paperwork, read all the medical jargon, and said, "She had a tough start, but everything looks good. She is doing great!"

We were beyond relieved. Now we could breathe, and allow ourselves to tear open the envelope and see the photo of our new baby girl. It was more than love at first sight because we were in love with her even before we opened that envelope. We chose for her American name to be Olivia Gwendolyn Park Murphy.

It is strange to think that there was a moment of doubt about accepting a baby into our family due to medical problems. I truly can't imagine we would have passed on her, but the situation did create a moment of doubt and fear. We had waited so long and gone through so much to be able to have a family, and we wanted it to be a happy and healthy one. That is why we waited to look at her photo until *after* we knew the situation. Once we saw her it would become personal and we would be even more connected than we already were. We loved her the moment we heard about her, but once we saw her face we became deeply and madly in love with this baby a world away.

It seemed the wait for our Olivia was so much longer. Everything with Maddie had gone faster than we anticipated, but the timing with Olivia made it a slower process. The Korean government shuts down pretty much all of December until the New Year. Which means, so does everything with adoptions.

One day in January, I sat on the steps crying. I was so eager for our baby to come home to us. The anticipation seemed so much harder this time around.

Maddie, who was only three at the time, found me there crying and asked, "What's wrong, Mommy?" I told her I was sad because I was so excited for her new baby sister, and it was hard to be patient.

She gave me a hug, and said, "She will be here soon."

I was amazed by how those words and that hug calmed my spirit. My toddler had reminded me that our family would come together soon enough, but for now, I needed to stop moping around and enjoy the little one who was standing beside me. Soon I would be juggling the blessed challenge of being a mommy of two.

In mid-February, after playing phone tag with the social worker at Children's Home, we finally got the information we had been waiting for. Olivia would be with us the following week. Maddie had her "Big Sister" shirt set out along with a stuffed pink bunny to bring to her new sister. Olivia, who is now twelve, still snuggles with her "Gotcha Day" gift from her big sister.

We were all gathered at the airport once again. This time we had even more friends and family with us. Last time had gone so smoothly, we thought it was safe to bring more people along. Because this was after the 9/11 attacks, our experience at the airport was quite different. We had to wait in the baggage claim area just outside the international gate. They held her up to the window from the second story so all of us down below could get a glimpse of her. Then we had to wait a few more agonizing minutes for all the paperwork in customs to be completed before we could see her and hold her.

She was crying inconsolably. The Korean escort kept telling me to "bop her bottom," assuring me that the bopping of the bottom would calm her down. I had no such luck. I walked the baggage claim area alone, bouncing her as I spoke and sang to her, trying my best to soothe her. I tried feeding her a bottle. Nothing worked.

I could only imagine how this small baby felt after such a long flight. She was thrust into a new country, with new smells and new people who all looked so foreign. Everything she had become accustomed to in her short lifetime was gone. She didn't understand that we would be her new normal. She couldn't comprehend that these were the people who would love her forever, and she would be our greatest love right beside her sister.

When we got home, I changed her diaper and realized that the source of her crankiness was very likely an upset stomach. After I put her in clean clothes and gave her a warm bottle, she seemed to come around. We even caught a glimpse of a smile.

Maddie was all over her. She loved her instantaneously and wanted to be part of everything. The first couple of weeks of getting her acclimated to the time change was a bit more challenging than they had been with Maddie. It was a little trickier this time around because we had another little girl to take care of. I'm not ashamed to admit that under the persuasion of severe sleep deprivation, I questioned whether or not Mike and I were capable of being parents to two children. (I know those of you with three or more kids took a break from reading this to roll your eyes.) Luckily, we soon realized that we could handle the juggle of parenting more than one child and we settled into the peace of knowing that this was our perfect family.

Months later, I sat outside watching the girls playing together. It was sweet, and I wished I could have bottled that moment up and tucked it away in a safe place where I could come back and live it again and again. As I watched them playing so nicely, I had what you might call an "aha moment." I reflected back on the decision I had made years before to place my baby boy up for adoption and how angry I had been at God for all the years of infertility. I realized in a single moment that God wasn't punishing me with infertility for the decision I had made. He was showing me the beautiful gift of being on the receiving end of adoption. He was allowing me to know firsthand how wonderful it feels to be given that gift. He *really* did know what He was doing. I wasn't being punished. I was being rewarded—not once, but twice.

CHAPTER NINE
Facebook

"As much as you want to plan your life, it has a way of surprising you with unexpected things that will make you happier than you originally planned. That is what you call God's will."
—Unknown

SOCIAL MEDIA IS A FUNNY thing. It is a product of the times through which we divulge bits and pieces of our lives with the world. It is a glimpse into someone's world through a computer screen. Some people are very private and some put it all out there. Some people may say it is a waste of time, a vortex filled with useless games and people sharing images of what they ate for dinner. It took me down a road I knew I would someday venture, but never knew when. It was a new direction that would change my life for the better and open up a whole new realm of emotions. Some of these feelings I had tucked away for more than twenty years.

It all began when I typed a specific name into the search bar on Facebook. I had typed this same name time and time again through all sorts of search engines. My results would either be a million hits or nothing at all. This time was different. What happened after I typed in the familiar name took my breath away. Up popped one name, one person, one face. There wasn't the typical list of people to narrow down. It was simply *him*.

Could it really be? I scanned the birth date and read June 16, 1987. It *had* to be him. My pulse rocketed from a standard resting rate to that of an Olympic runner in a matter of seconds. It was the same birth date, and he had similar features. Two familiar eyes looked back at me from the image of a complete stranger. A flood of emotions overtook me: excitement, anxiousness, sadness, happiness.

It was Joshua, the baby I had carried in my womb for nine months, but had never met. Now the name I had thought about every day of my life had a face. Although it was a face I had never seen before, it was so familiar to me. A warm smile and gentle eyes looked back at me. For so many years, I had referred to him as "the baby" I had and chose adoption for, but now he was a young man. There was a face to the name, which washed away "the baby" label. There was a calmness about him that helped ease the anxiety boiling inside of me.

For a moment, I was paralyzed by my emotions. It's funny how a single photo can make your heart fill with more love than you could possibly imagine. I experienced that two other times with my daughters, and twenty years after making the most difficult decision of my life, I experienced it again with my son. It's a feeling I cannot adequately put into words. The best way I can describe it is beautiful, warm, and endearing.

As I looked at his profile picture, trying to take it all in, I noticed we had one mutual friend. My heart skipped a beat. Who could I know who also knows my son? I looked closely at the profile picture of our common friend. It was my next-door neighbor! This girl, whom I had known since she was eight and was now a senior in high school, was someone I had watched grow into a smart, beautiful young woman.

She was the girl I trusted to stay with my children when Mike and I needed a sitter. Over the years, she had become like a daughter to me, coming to me for advice about boys and telling me things I had to swear to secrecy.

Because we had such a nice relationship, I knew I could trust her with the news of my discovery. So again, through the beauty of modern technology, I whipped out my cell phone and texted her.

"How do you know Joshua?"

Like most eighteen-year-olds, she texted back with lightning speed and said, "I work with him. How do *you* know him?"

Well, there wasn't enough character space or time to text back that answer. Besides, it wasn't really a text message type of story. It was more of a face-to-face story to tell. So I invited her over.

I felt a sense of relief that out of all the people I knew in Joshua's age range, *she* was the connection. I knew I could tell her my story, and she would understand and keep it between us until I knew what to do next. So I sat her down on my bed that night and told her the whole story. She was shocked and happy all at the same time. I told her she couldn't say anything, especially not to Joshua. I also apologized for putting her in an awkward situation. But I trusted her, just as she had trusted me so many times before.

Over the next few weeks I visited Joshua's Facebook page every day. I even got up enough nerve to follow him on Twitter. I figured people have a lot of followers on Twitter so I wouldn't stick out. I also noticed he went to the same school as my niece, Leslie. What a small world! I wondered if they ever ran into each other, and if so, maybe she thought he looked familiar to her. There were so many coincidences and common threads, it made me smile. In a sense, it allowed me to get to know him from a safe distance.

It was hard to pinpoint the exact emotions I was feeling, but it was a comforting combination of relief, happiness, peace, and closure all swirled together. He seemed like a wonderful young man, and I found myself wanting to meet him.

I cried to Mike and told him, "This is huge, and I have so many emotions. How do I take this in and make sense of it all?"

I wondered if this was a sign from God that it was the right time for me to reach out to Joshua. Could He be trying to tell me that it was time for me to finally meet my son? I had written a letter to Joshua when he turned sixteen, but I never sent it, although writing it felt very therapeutic at the time. Looking back, I'm glad I never sent it. Sixteen can be such a hard age even without throwing in a letter from your long-lost birth mother on top of all the emotional, social, and hormonal changes. I couldn't do that to him. But he was older now, and I thought maybe this young man would be ready to know me.

I spent many nights lying in my bed wondering what he knew about me. Did he even know about me at all? If he did, what emotions did the thought of me stir up inside of him? Anger, confusion, curiosity?

I had so much to think about. Now that I knew who he was and where he was, what would I do? If I did anything at all, *how* would I do it? The only thing I knew for certain was I needed to put my son's feelings and life first, just as I had twenty-two years before.

CHAPTER TEN
The Letter

"If you are brave enough to say good-bye, life will reward you with a new hello."
—Unknown

I REMEMBER AS A CHILD I was always so excited when the mail came. I would run out to get it and be thrilled if I got a letter. Today we want the instant gratification of a response *now*. When someone takes a day or two to respond to an e-mail, we wonder if they could be sick, out of town, or perhaps their computer or phone isn't working. We live in a time when people can always get in touch with you. Even while on vacation, we can still receive e-mails from work. Before modern technology, when our friends or family went on vacation, we hoped for a postcard with an image of the far-off place they were visiting and a few handwritten words on the back telling us they were having a great time.

It was a simpler time that I sometimes miss, when people took the time to sit down with paper and pen to write a letter. They carved out a chunk of time and purposefully wrote a well-thought-out message. It was truly a planned act. They were committing time exclusively to the person to whom they were writing.

I needed to write an important letter. I needed to carve quiet time out of my day and purposefully write this letter with thought and emotion. It needed to convey the proper tone and feelings. I wanted it to be mailed, delivered, and received so it could be held in the hands of those reading it—so it could be tangible and real. I decided to type it with a handwritten font because I knew I would be writing and rewriting the words until they were perfect, and I wanted to eliminate the need to crumple up dozens of sheets of paper and start all over. It seemed more logical to backspace and retype, which I did a lot.

I needed this letter to be perfect. This one piece of paper with my heartfelt words could change my life. I had to write to Joshua's parents. Since Pat was raising him, locating them was easy. I guess that little piece was part of a bigger plan too.

It was a hard letter to write on so many levels, and yet so easy on others. I had twenty-two years' worth of feelings that had been folded up and neatly tucked away as I spent that part of my life holding on to the knowledge that the boy I had chosen adoption for was safe, loved, and cared for. So many emotions came pouring out, along with lots of tears.

I had to choose my words carefully. I knew it would be a shock to hear from me after so many years, and perhaps it would even be a little scary. I was confident that they would not jump for joy when they received it. I needed to reassure them that I didn't want to disrupt the harmony of their family. I didn't even know if Joshua knew about me. After all, he was a baby when his dad had gotten married, and Pat's wife was the only mother he had ever known. I realized they could easily have not told him.

I wanted them to understand that I was not the same eighteen-year-old girl who was scared, pregnant, and not ready to be a mom. I had matured into a woman who was now a mother of two daughters who were, ironically, adopted. Most importantly, I needed his mom to know that *she* was his mother. I was merely his "belly mom." *She* had raised him, changed his diapers, witnessed his first steps, kissed his owies, and taught him how to love and be kind. She deserved and earned the title of Mom. I wasn't hoping to "take over" or have him choose a family.

I told them of all the strange coincidences—or "God blinks" as my friend calls them. I explained that I took them as a sign I was ready to make the move to get in touch. I simply wanted to meet the boy I had thought of every day of his life. I felt like I was ready, but if they had decided not to tell him about me, I would respect their decision. *They* were his parents and knew what was best for *their* son.

I finished my letter, clicked on the "save as" tab, and closed the file. A month later I went back to the file, tweaked it, and hit "save" again. Another month went by, and I had a little more time to think it through. I decided that I was ready to make the next move. I hit "Print" and handwrote my information on the page. I folded it carefully, addressed the envelope, and put a stamp on it. My hand trembled and my heart raced as I placed it in the mailbox.

Every day after, I wondered, "Did they receive it yet?" I constantly looked at Joshua's Facebook page for clues. I felt like a bit of a stalker in some ways, but I thought if his parents had received the letter and discussed it with him, he might post something. Then one day, I read, "A weird weekend. I have a lot to think and pray about." I wondered if it might be related to my letter. Had his parents shared it with him? I had no way of knowing for certain. My anxiety settled into hope.

A week or so passed. I had fallen asleep watching TV one night on the couch. I was feeling a bit under the weather and needed to drag myself upstairs to bed, but I decided I would give Facebook and e-mail one last scan before I went

up. I had one new message on Facebook. When I saw who it
was from, I did a double take and ran to get Mike.

There it was—a message from my son. This was the
moment I had always wondered about. The very thing I had
dreamed about time and again was represented by a small
red flag on my Facebook page. Glowing on my computer
screen were the first words my son would ever say to me—a
few simple words that would change my life forever.

> *May 11 at 10:25 p.m.*
>
> *Hello,*
>
> *I have been thinking this through for around 2
> weeks. I've always wondered when this part of my
> life would come around. I knew that eventually I
> would have an opportunity to meet you, I just never
> had a clue as to when. I am a mixture of excitement
> and stress. When my parents told me that you had
> written them a letter it took 2 full days for it to
> register. I immediately knew that I was going to get
> in touch and eventually meet you. I just needed to
> pray about it to make sure I did it in the best way.
> After I did that I started piecing things together,
> Jenn and Leslie and you following me on Twitter
> and what not. I was a little shocked that I didn't put
> it all together sooner but then again I didn't see this
> coming haha. I would really like to talk via email or
> Facebook or whatever is easiest for now. Meeting
> you might be a little overwhelming for me at this
> point. I have a lot of questions as I'm sure you do
> too. I'm a fairly transparent person so don't be
> afraid to ask the tougher stuff if you need to.*
>
> *Joshua*

CHAPTER ELEVEN
E-mails and Emotions

*"She knew she could never go back and make some of the details pretty.
All she could do was move forward and make the whole beautiful."*
—Terri St. Cloud

TO ME, AN E-MAIL IS MORE than a simple exchange of words between computers. It is the giving and taking of personal information that allows you to get to know a person. Through this modern form of communication, we can tell stories full of emotion and build a foundation for a relationship to grow. It allows us to exchange information in a way that feels safer than a face-to-face exchange. Sentences can be written, and if they don't sound quite right, they can be deleted and rewritten. There is no need to fumble over words or worry that nerves may cause something you want to say to come out wrong. It was the perfect way for me and my son to get to know one another.

After receiving my first e-mail from Joshua, I spent the weeks to follow exchanging messages back and forth. We had decided this was the safest and most comfortable way to go about it. We shared the same feelings of excitement and nervousness.

How on earth could I take twenty-two years of feelings, thoughts, and questions and casually send them off to the son I've loved but never known? How would I e-mail a first impression of myself? It was more than a little overwhelming. I wondered how I would properly convey my emotions and heartfelt stories by writing them in black 12-point font against a white screen. The smiley face composed of a colon and right parenthetical only goes so far. But I was determined to try.

I strained over every word and sentence, hoping to make each one perfectly convey my thoughts. We exchanged random things about ourselves—both serious and silly. It was like a game of Twenty Questions at first. We shared our basic likes and dislikes, and details about our lives and families.

He lived in the same town I did, the town his father had grown up in. I wondered if we had ever crossed paths at some point in time without realizing it. We both shared a similar sense of humor and love for creativity. We enjoyed some of the same TV shows and foods. He was the oldest in his family of two sisters and one brother, as well as the oldest of all his cousins.

I told him that someday I would love to tell him my side of the story about everything. Not that my story was different than what his father had told him, but it was *mine*—with *my* thoughts and *my* emotions. That piece of the puzzle felt like it might be better shared in person, but he didn't want to wait to hear it. So I sat down at my emotionless keyboard and turned the black and white of my computer screen into a story full of honesty and tears, hoping that all the feeling I put into it wouldn't get lost in the blandness of the monitor he would be reading it on.

It felt so good to finally tell him my thoughts and feelings behind all the decisions I made when I was eighteen. I was able to tell him that every choice I made was done in the hopes of doing what I thought was best for him. I wondered what he had been told and what he had thought about me for all those years.

Joshua told me he learned that his mom wasn't his birth mother at a very young age, when he was six or seven. His father felt he had to tell Joshua at that time because a family member had shared the information with his young child. It was likely only a matter of time before the news would get to Joshua. That piece of information made me wonder what and when his parents would have told him about me if they hadn't been forced to tell him at such a young age.

His mom was *his mom* and that should have been all that mattered, but he told me he had a difficult time with separation anxiety for a while. I can't imagine that pain and confusion in a young boy's life.

Joshua's adoption experience was different than that of my girls. They were Korean and their adoptions were always openly discussed in our home. We explained that they came from their "belly mom" to be with us from the very beginning; they never knew any differently. But for Joshua to hear that the mom he had always known as his mother wasn't his "belly mom" was a shock he never saw coming. How could such a young boy possibly understand that?

In his teen years, Joshua said he began to use that knowledge to hurt his mom by saying things like, "You aren't my *real* mom!" That would be a gut punch for any mother. But teens say things in anger at their parents because they know it will hit them where it hurts. Joshua told me his biggest regret was ever saying those words to his mother.

I wanted him to know that choosing to give him up for adoption was the greatest sacrifice I had ever made or would make. He needed to know I chose that because I loved him so much—not because I didn't love him enough. It had nothing to do with wanting him or not, it had to do with wanting what he *needed*, which was always the most important thing to me.

The e-mail I got in response from him made me feel like all my decisions were the right ones at the time, and that I had answered some pretty heavy questions he had. He reassured me that he did have the wonderful life I had always wanted for him, with a wonderful family. I spent all those years wondering how he was, and now I finally knew that the entire time, he was well! The part that surprised me was that he had grown into this wonderful person who let me open up to him and tell *my* story without judgment.

He wasn't mad or angry; he was simply thankful to have questions about his life answered. What a gift. Our e-mail exchanges also answered my questions about how he was, what he knew, and how he felt about it all today. All the heavy stuff was on the table. I found myself checking my e-mail all the time, anxiously waiting for the next message from him.

After a couple of weeks, Joshua decided he was ready to finally meet. It was time for me to see my son face to face—to look into his eyes for the first time, to finally hug the child I had carried in my womb for nine months, but never touched. I had dreamed of this moment since the day he was born, and I was ready.

CHAPTER TWELVE
Coffee Shop

"It's exciting when you find parts of yourself in someone else."
—Curiano.com

I WAS OVER THE MOON with excitement. I told Joshua to pick the time and place, and I would be there. I wondered where we would meet that was a neutral location—maybe a park or restaurant? When he suggested a coffee shop near my house, I was thrilled. Our meeting was set for Saturday, May 29—a date I will always remember.

The week leading up to our get-together seemed to move so slowly, and our meeting was on my mind all the time. I decided to put together a gift for him—a box with personal things. I had a copy of the letter I wrote to him when he turned sixteen that I never sent, a copy of the letter I sent to his parents, a few pictures of a younger me, a dinosaur PEZ because he told me he always liked dinosaurs and I thought it was a fun token of childhood, and a copy of *Life's Little Instruction Book* with certain quotes and pictures highlighted. I filled it with items that would make him laugh, think, and feel loved. I wanted him to know I had thought about him every day of his life, even though I wasn't with him all those years.

May 29 couldn't come fast enough. I felt an indescribable mixture of excitement and nervousness. I couldn't eat or sleep. I surrounded myself that week with tasks to complete, friends to hang out with, busy stuff that would make each day go by quickly without much thought. I suppose it was a bit like the "nesting" phase an expectant mother goes through as she prepares to meet her unborn child for the first time.

When the day finally arrived, I was thankful for my goddaughter's third birthday party in the morning. The joy of celebrating her special day helped take my mind off my nerves. Despite the party, the swirl of anxiety and excitement made me too nervous to eat or drink. I even turned down cake. After the party, I stopped by my house, gathered my thoughts, and decided I would go early, hoping my nerves would settle once I got there. I had *never* been so nervous for anything in my life.

My girls asked where I was going and why they couldn't come along. I told them I was meeting with a friend and wasn't sure when I would be home. Mike, knowing what a nervous wreck I was, assured me he would distract them, and they would have fun while I was gone.

My plan was to go ten minutes early so I could get settled on the couch, rather than the sterile table and chairs, and watch for him. When I got there, the couch was taken—by Joshua. I walked over to the couch where he sat reading a book.

"So you came early too," I said, breaking the ice. He stood up, tall like his father. I asked if it would be weird if I gave him a hug, and he said "no." So I did, and for the first time ever, I held my son. For a moment, time stood still, and my heart overflowed with all the love I had stored up for twenty-two years.

For the first few minutes, it seemed that we both looked at each other in disbelief. I kept thinking how strangely awesome this moment was. Looking into my son's eyes for the first time felt so familiar. I realized it was because they were just like mine. We also had the same smile. We spent the next three hours laughing and getting to know one another.

I asked him if this would be the start of a relationship or closure for him. He wanted to go forward with this new relationship and take our time with it. We were on the same page. Although I am an inpatient planner, and this was really the first time in my life when I had to slow down and be truly thoughtful with each decision, surprisingly this came easily to me. I had waited so long for this and was not going to screw it up by being overly excited and anxious.

I asked if we could take a picture together. The photo we took that day is displayed on my fridge and in my family room. When we walked out together, we hugged each other and said our good-byes. I was on such an emotional high. There are no words that could adequately articulate how it felt to be able to meet him and talk to him. How do you describe hugging your grown son for the first time? It was a lot like holding my girls at the airport for the first time—best described as an out-of-body experience.

Joshua was such a warm, lovely, polite, put-together young man. I couldn't help but think of his mom and dad. They had raised a great son. I was beyond thankful to finally meet him and be in his life after so many years. I realized his dad really had known what was best for our baby when he fought for custody. If I had "won" and Joshua had been adopted by strangers, I may have never found him. I could have missed out on knowing him at all. Once again, God knew what He was doing.

It was interesting to think of the concept of nature verses nurture after our meeting. I could see so much of myself in Joshua. My daughters, whom I had nurtured from the time they were just babies, obviously have none of my physical traits, but this young man did. There was something comforting in seeing a bit of myself in him. It made sense that he would have some of my physical traits, but he seemed to have also inherited my creativity, sense of humor, and ease of conversation.

That meeting in the coffee shop was truly one of the best moments of my life. It ranks on the same level as the day I married my husband and the first time I held my two beautiful daughters. It was a day that changed my life. Now, it was time for me to share my story with my daughters.

CHAPTER THIRTEEN
Telling the Girls

"Motherhood is not a battle against other mothers. Motherhood is YOUR journey with YOUR children."
—Unknown

I HADN'T MENTIONED anything about Joshua to my daughters. I wasn't sure if he and I meeting would be closure for him or the start of something new. I knew that I would respect whatever he decided. I so wanted the girls to know about him, but I didn't want to explain the whole story prematurely. When I knew Joshua and I were on the same page, I began to think about how and when to tell my girls.

At one point, my mom asked if I had said anything to the girls yet. I told her I was waiting to see what developed after meeting Joshua. She mentioned that the girls could probably sense something was different with me. Looking back, I'm sure I seemed like a bit of a wreck to them. Typically, they had my undivided attention, but for a while, my mind was spinning with thoughts of Joshua, and I was more emotional than usual.

My mom pointed out that my daughters were the perfect children with whom to share my story. They would eventually be curious about their own birth mothers, and this was a good way to help them understand. Adoption was always, and still is, an open item of discussion in our home, so I knew in some respects, it would be easy to tell them.

I sat both girls down on my bed and searched for the perfect words. I explained that some women could have a baby in their belly but not be old enough or feel capable of being a mommy. Other women couldn't have a baby in their belly but were old enough and felt ready for motherhood. And some women could be both physically capable and mentally ready to have a baby in their belly *and* be a mother. I explained that their belly moms weren't old enough or ready to be a mom, so they had an adoption plan—a plan to let their babies go to be with us so we could be their parents. I told them at the time my body wasn't capable of having a baby in my belly. The girls seemed to understand all that quite easily, but then I had to describe the slightly more complicated part of my situation.

I explained that there was a time when I did have a baby in my belly, but I was too young to be the best mommy I could be. I wanted the baby to have a wonderful life, one that I wasn't prepared to give. I wasn't married, and I knew there were other families out there who couldn't physically have their own child, and who would give my baby everything I was unable to.

I asked them if they remembered being upset with me a few weeks before when I went to have coffee with a special friend and wouldn't allow them to come along. I explained that I was meeting the baby I had given up for adoption, and that he was twenty-two years old now. They had a big brother of sorts. They were happy and excited, but quiet. At the time, they were only nine and six. I'm certain in their quiet joy, they were trying to find a way to comprehend it all. I'm sure they also wondered how a baby got into my belly in the first place. I'm thankful they wondered that in silence. I'm not sure I could have braved the birds and bees conversation on top of everything else.

That night, as I was putting the girls to bed, I asked if they had any questions.

Olivia said, "No. I think it's neat."

Maddie said, "Yes."

I braced myself for a question that had been so deep and personal, she'd been too afraid to ask before—one that likely weighed heavily on her mind as she worked up the courage to speak the words aloud to me.

"Do you think he likes spaghetti?"

Phew! I got to dodge the "how did he get in your belly" question for a little while longer. I asked her why she wanted to know.

She replied, "If he does, we would have something in common."

Hidden in the middle of her simple question was a search for a connection with Joshua. My heart was full.

A few weeks later, my neighbor Jenn was graduating high school and having an open house. Joshua was going to be there, also. I figured it would be a good time for Mike and the girls to meet him without the pressure and worry that might come with a formal gathering. It would be a nice, casual setting with no expectations.

We were inside getting food, and I pointed him out to them.

He casually broke the ice by saying, "Hi! I'm Josh."

My daughters and I sat at a table with Jenn, Josh, and some others who all worked with them. Some of them had also babysat my girls. They were giving him the inside scoop on Maddie and Olivia—like how he should never play Candyland with Olivia because she cheats, and Maddie makes up her own rules when it comes to board games, and life in general. It was surreal to realize that this was only the second time I had ever seen Joshua, and there I was listening to these young adults so candidly tell him about my family. It was such a perfect and stress-free way for him to get to know us. God was working even in the casual conversations at a high school graduation party.

That summer, Joshua came to our home for dinner one night. I felt so nervous. So many questions played through my mind. What would he think of us? How would the girls react? Is the house clean enough? Do I look nice enough? They were all the silly things that I now realize didn't matter. It was the start to a wonderful, new family dynamic. We would get together more often, and it became more comfortable and easy. It felt natural.

One day when Joshua was over at the house, Olivia was trying to ask him something, but she couldn't get the words right. She wanted to know if he was her *brother*. They both had the same "mom." I was his "belly mom," and I was her "forever mom." It was such a confusing concept. There was absolutely no blood relation, yet they were family. Josh had become part of *our* family, but at the same time he had *his* family. And while our families were separate, in some ways we were also all connected. I couldn't fully wrap my head around it all. There was no clear-cut definition for it—no defined roles. This page in life's playbook completely lacked prescribed rules.

It was as if I had been playing Monopoly for the past forty years, and my little silver top hat had been picked up and set down on a LIFE game board. While the silver top hat works well in a game of Monopoly, it doesn't quite fit in with the plastic station wagons filled with pink and blue pegs in a game of LIFE. If the game pieces get mixed up while you're playing board games, it is easy to fix. You simply organize them and put them back in their rightful places—you *just put that top hat back where it goes*. But when your game piece ends up on someone else's board in the real game of life, it's not as easy to fix.

I knew where I belonged. I belonged with my family— my husband and my two daughters. But I also wanted to be part of Joshua's game. And I wanted Joshua's game piece to be in both *my* family's game with *his* family's game. But the rules, game pieces, and game boards were all so different from one another.

I wondered if it would it be possible for Joshua and me to make a smooth transition between game boards. I was good at my game and welcomed new pieces—especially the "birth son" piece. My game, and all its parts, welcomed the new piece. My concern was if his game could let me in. I wasn't sure what would be expected of me, or what my role would be. I worried about what would be too much and what might seem like not enough. Would the other pieces in his game accept me? I wasn't sure if his family could allow me to be part of the life they had created.

If I was feeling this way, I imagined my husband, my daughters, and Joshua felt the same. It was a whole new game board with no rules and no directions. There was no assembly instruction pamphlet. We could only make it up as we went. We would learn what works and what doesn't. We would choose to play this game of life before the timer runs out and hope that we played it fully.

CHAPTER FOURTEEN
Feelings Unleashed

"Sometimes, you just can't tell anybody how you really feel. Not because you don't know why. Not because you don't know your purpose. Not because you don't trust them. But because you can't find the right words to make them understand."
—Unknown

I LOVE THE QUOTE:

"What screws us up the most in life is the picture in our heads of how it is supposed to be…"

I'm not sure who first said it, but when I came across it, I thought it made so much sense. I now realize, as I relive this whole journey through writing, that I have suppressed so many feelings. I had a plan as a young girl of how my life would go, and when the plan that I pictured didn't pan out, I ended up with a lot of feelings I wasn't sure how to handle. So I took them like a sweater and folded them neatly, then placed them in a mental drawer to deal with later. But now, all the feelings I had being a scared pregnant teen up to my present-day emotions that have come from reconnecting with my son, have resurfaced.

Instead of dealing with the feelings associated with having a baby and placing him for adoption, I stayed focused on the plan my parents and I had made. I knew in my heart it was the right decision. I had to detach myself from the emotional part of it so I could carry through with my plan. I put certain walls up to protect myself—walls that I am still working at knocking down today.

I probably should have seen a therapist or talked to someone to get those feelings out of the drawer and deal with them, but I didn't. I had buried them so deeply, I didn't even know I had them. All those years, I thought I was okay, and I had moved on. I thought about my baby all the time. But I never *felt* the emotion attached to those thoughts. I think that is why, until I met Joshua, I always referred to him as "the baby." Even though I knew his name, I never allowed myself to call him that because giving "the baby" a name, would make the situation feel more *real*. To cope, I had put up a wall, even around my child's name.

My struggle to hold a new baby is an example of one wall I've put up. I'm good when it comes to my nieces and nephews, but when friends have a new baby I get a feeling of panic over the thought of holding their infant. I'm sure I come across as rude or as if I have ice running through my veins, but it's not that at all. I love babies, and I love the people in my life who have had babies. I think because I never held Joshua or my daughters as newborns, I panic. I don't know how to *feel*. I wonder sometimes if I'm still angry that I couldn't have my own babies at the right time. Or perhaps I regret not holding Joshua and saying a proper "good-bye." I could be unconsciously jealous that it is not *my* newborn. Whatever the reason, it is a wall I am trying to knock down.

After I found Joshua on Facebook, I had a face to go with the name. Only then could I call him Joshua and allow myself to begin to feel. It made him seem *real*. Having a face to go with his name, and seeing how much that face resembled my own, was an odd, eerie, and wonderful feeling. It was a feeling that warmed my soul and took over my world. When I first reached out to Joshua's parents, I honestly didn't think I had maternal feelings toward him, in part because I was really just meeting him. He was truly a stranger to me, still a mystery—an overwhelmingly beautiful mystery.

The more we e-mailed back and forth, and the more we discovered how much we had in common, the more my feelings grew. After we met, those feelings became stronger. As months passed into years, Josh became part of our family, and the maternal instinct I had pushed down for so many years surfaced. I had always loved him in a way that made me want to protect him, which was why I made the choice to give him a better life through adoption, a sacrifice that came from the huge love I had for him even before I knew him.

As we got better acquainted, I fell in love with Joshua. It was like when a mother holds her child for the first time and sees her own eyes looking back at her. It was that kind of falling in love with a piece of myself in another human being. It was that maternal love that allowed me call him my *son*, not "the baby" or even Joshua, but son. The son I had carried in my womb for nine months. The son I loved so much that I was willing to accept my inability to give him the childhood he deserved. Even as I call him "my son," I know it is different than his mother calling him the same because she raised him, and I respect that so much.

Sometimes after people have met Joshua, they say to me, "You have an awesome son." And I absolutely agree, yet by saying "thank you" or "I know" I feel as though I am taking something away from his parents. That is a hard and unsettling feeling to deal with. The fact is, I can only take credit for part of him—the part that created him and gave him life. Of course that is a huge piece of who he is, but so is the part that shaped him into this wonderful young man he has become. His parents are responsible for that, and for that, I am grateful.

There were so many new feelings I was experiencing, and I wasn't sure how to make sense of them all. Then two years ago, a friend introduced me to an adoption support group with Catholic Charities. It's ironic that the very first place I went to as a young pregnant teen was Catholic Charities, and then decades later, I was back for the support the organization could offer.

This group is filled with birth mothers and adoptees. There are many different ages, generations, and stories. Some of these women have nice stories of reunions and forgiveness; others share their anger and resentment and feelings of disconnect and loneliness. I feel as though my story falls under the category of reunion and forgiveness. But in hearing all the other stories, I realize I have so many feelings that are surfacing now, more than twenty-eight years after giving my son up for adoption.

I wish I'd had this group all along. It may have helped me deal with the surprise of the feelings that seemed to pop up out of the blue. I was bombarded by a whole range of feelings, from anger and hurt to happiness and peace. When other women told their stories and expressed the feelings they were struggling with, I found myself crying because I was having those feelings, too. The drawer where I had stored my neatly folded emotions opens wider each time I attend a meeting. My feelings come unfolded and lie in a heap out in the open. Most of the time, the sensation catches me off guard.

It is good to feel the emotions—all of them—the happiness, sadness, anger, and grief. By feeling all the different emotions associated with my story of being a birth mother, I become a better mother to my daughters. I can tell them the thoughts their birth mothers had, and it can bring peace to them when they wonder. I can tell them *I know* how their birth moms felt when they made the difficult decision to place them up for adoption. I can tell them with certainty that *they are* thought of and loved and never forgotten by the mothers who gave them life. One day my daughters will want to take the journey to find their birth mothers, and I will be with them every step of the way, through every emotion, question, and fear.

Part of dealing with all these new feelings and emotions is allowing my family to feel and process their emotions on this journey, as well. While I was a scared pregnant teen fighting for the perfect plan for my baby, my parents were my support and my rock. But this time around, I wasn't really feeling the love and support I had experienced all those years ago. This really took a toll on me. I was taking out this anger, confusion, and sadness in other areas of my life. I had the sense that through the journey of my reconnection with Joshua, my parents weren't really present. I wondered if they were worried that I wouldn't find the happy ending I was hoping for. Or perhaps they were simply in denial of the reality of what was happening. I wasn't sure what was causing their uneasiness about my reconnection with my birth son, but I knew I had to find out.

It is never easy when you have to go to your parents about something that makes you feel unhappy. But it was a long-overdue conversation. When I sat down with them, all my tears, anger, and sadness came pouring out. I was angry that they never asked about Joshua. I was hurt they never asked how I was doing during the early stages of the reunion. How could my mom rant about the cable company so much in four years and barely even ask her daughter about this life-changing event?

My mom is not a head-in-the-sand type of woman. She is honest, says it like it is, and feels emotions bigger and more than the average person. She dislikes no one. She can tear up over something she saw on NBC's *Today Show*. She is always there to talk to about anything and always plays both sides to help her children understand the opposite viewpoint. But she wasn't showing me that side of herself during the time I was becoming acquainted with Joshua, and that hurt.

I knew deep down it wasn't because they didn't care. I had to acknowledge that maybe they hadn't moved beyond the change in plans we all agreed on for this baby. I *had* moved forward. I had forgiven Joshua's dad, and I realized God was in control all along. I fell maternally in love with my son as I slowly got to know him, and he became part of our family.

My parents hadn't had that opportunity. They felt it was my time to do that. Now that I had, I wanted to share him with the people who had supported me the most during my pregnancy, my parents. I wanted them to get to know him like I did. I wanted them to see the similarities. I wasn't sure what their role was in this transition, but I didn't believe we needed to define roles. I just knew Joshua was an important part of my life, and I wanted to share him with the other important people in my life.

CHAPTER FIFTEEN
Dual Citizenship

"We know a mother and father can love more than one child, so why is it so hard to understand that a child can love more than one mother and father?"
—Unknown

WHEN I THINK ABOUT adoption, I think of all the people in this world who have dual citizenship. They are citizens of the country in which they were born but also have citizenship in a country where they make their home. They love spending time in both countries—one is not better than the other. They love both for different reasons and maybe both countries have similar characteristics.

When couples get married, they marry into a second family. When there is divorce and remarriage, it creates a whole new family. Most of the time we embrace these new families. In such situations, these individuals have a "dual citizenship" of sorts. They are members of two different families. These situations are prevalent in our society. They have become much less the exception to the typical family structure and more of the norm. I wonder then, when you are talking about adoption and reuniting, why can't it be that easy or uncomplicated? Perhaps in some situations it is, but more often than not, these reunions seem to elicit a sense of fear, anxiety, and even anger.

I have had Joshua in my life for over five years now. He has his family, his parents, his siblings, and extended relatives. That is his "home country," where his allegiance is, and rightfully so. His first priority and his loyalty is to *his* family. They are who he spends holidays and other important dates with. I love that even though his siblings are all adults, they carve out special days to spend together doing fun things as a family.

On the flip side, I also have my family—my husband and my daughters. I have my parents, siblings, nieces, and nephews. My allegiance is to them, as it should be. But as Joshua and I entered each other's lives, I found myself seriously wondering, what happens when our two worlds collide? Is it possible to share the love?

The first time my parents met Joshua was at Mike's fiftieth birthday party. It was a bustling gathering of friends and family, filled with music and commotion. It was not a grand meeting of the family. In some regards it was very casual and left no time for awkwardness or for anyone to feel uncomfortable in an obvious way. The first thing my dad said to Joshua, as he side-hugged him with a pat on the shoulder—the way guys do—was, "You're one lucky son of a bitch to have so many people love you."

Those words, although not exactly eloquent, resonated with both Joshua and myself. They also made me think. Joshua has never been put in a position to choose a family, pick a side, or pick a mother. We all knew our rightful places. Instead he gained this whole new family. Quite simply, there were now more people in his life to love and care about him. How could that be a bad thing? I don't believe it is.

I feel as though we are his second citizenship. We are that other country—a new, beautiful country that he visits and where he has a second home. He enjoys the food, the casual craziness of our culture, the people, and the love. He doesn't feel any less for his family, and at times, I believe it makes him appreciate his family even more in new ways. I also think he is learning to appreciate and learn about this new "country."

CHAPTER SIXTEEN
Present Day

"You don't always need a plan. Sometimes you just need to breathe, trust, let go, and see what happens."
—Unknown

IT HAS BEEN NEARLY SIX years since I first began this journey with Joshua. In that time, we have gotten to know one another in a wonderful way. God chose me to keep him safe and loved until he was ready to come into the world and make some couple very happy by completing their family.

Now, as adults, we have a close friendship. God has given us a second chance. A chance for us to have a relationship. A chance for me to share the love that has always been within me but had been tucked away, packed neatly in the drawers of my heart for decades. We can build our relationship without sacrificing the one he has with his mom and dad.

Mike and our daughters have welcomed him with open arms and hearts. The girls love having a "Big Bro," as they so lovingly call him. They wrestle, tease, and give each other a hard time. It is amusing, and fills my heart.

My siblings and their families have been around Joshua a few times, and everyone seems to hit it off and have a good time. Last year, for my forty-sixth birthday, my brother hosted a family get-together. It was the first time my whole family, including Joshua, was together. It was my best birthday ever.

Joshua was the first to arrive. He gave me flowers and a birthday card. It was the first gift he had ever given me. The card read, "Happy Birthday, Mom…I took a long, hard look in the mirror this morning, and just thought I'd tell you…nice job!" I can only imagine how he felt looking for a "mom" card that would fit our relationship, but he found the perfect one. It is a card I will keep forever, along with all the notes and cards I get from Maddie and Olivia.

As I look back at the path God has put me on, I see that it is so different than the plan I had as a little girl playing house in the backyard. So many parts of this journey were heartbreaking. Being a pregnant teen broke my parents' hearts and mine—each broken, but in their own way and for their own reasons. Living through the infertility roller coaster was heart wrenching for Mike and me, as we mourned what would never be. The adoption process was a test of our character and even more so a test in patience. Once all these separate paths came together on the twisting, bumpy road of life, my beautiful journey to motherhood became clear.

I never take for granted a single moment of motherhood. Of course, I have days like any other mom when I am frazzled and tired. But this full-circle journey to becoming a mom to Maddie and Olivia, and now Joshua, still takes my breath away when I sit back and think about it.

Today, I have a relationship with Joshua that is forever changing and growing into something wonderful. He has become part of my family. Somehow, through the twists and turns of life, I found motherhood—not in the way I had planned, but in exactly the perfectly imperfect way it was meant to happen.

"When you tell your story and it doesn't make you cry, you know you have healed."
—Unknown

EPILOGUE
In Their Own Words

"I wanted a perfect ending. Now I've learned, the hard way, that some poems don't rhyme, and some stories don't have a clear beginning, middle, and end. Life is about not knowing, having to change, taking the moment and making the best of it, without knowing what's going to happen next. Delicious ambiguity."
—Gilda Radner

From Joshua

IT TOOK ME SEVERAL months to work up to writing this. The story starts out kind of sad, and I didn't think that was a good way to kick off my addition to Jill's book, but it's the abridged version of what I went through growing up so it can't really be changed, I guess. The end of my little section is happy, I promise.

I was around seven years old when I was told about Jill. I wasn't even told what her name was—just that my mom wasn't my birth mom. I had a younger cousin who found out about it somehow, and she was a talker, so my parents decided it was better for me to hear it from them than to take a chance my cousin might tell me.

I didn't fully understand the situation. I was staring at a handful of baseball cards my dad had bought me earlier that day. I don't remember a lot from that time, but I do remember it was really hard for me to go to school after that. I spent several weeks of second-grade recess calling my mom and playing board games with the student counselor. I guess I just wanted to make sure she was still there.

As I got older, the idea of this "other mom" kept popping into my head. The usual kid questions of "Why didn't she want me?" and "Why did she fight to keep Dad from keeping me?" kept circling my brain. Because I couldn't answer those questions myself, I acted out. "You're not my real mom…" and "My other mom would let me do this…" were my go-to phrases for a few years when I was angry.

My teen years were pretty normal. I was your average angst-filled teenager and didn't think about my "other mom" very often. I even decided at one point that I didn't need to meet her. I had made up my mind that the family I had was all the family I needed.

Fast-forward through high school and a few years of college to when I was twenty-two. I get a phone call from my dad asking me to come to their house that evening. When I arrived, I was the only "kid" there—my younger brother and two younger sisters, who still lived there at the time, were gone. My mom had clearly been crying. I had no idea what to expect.

They sat me down and said they had received a letter from my birth mother asking if she could meet me. I was a little stunned, and that same feeling of not fully understanding set in. They handed me the letter and told me they wanted me to make that decision. They knew this day would eventually come, but I could tell they weren't ready for it. I spent the next few days talking with some of my close friends and family and praying about the best course of action. It was a weird few days. I even picked up smoking as a means of stress relief. (Don't be too worried—I have since quit.) I broke things off with a girl I had been seeing. I barely slept or ate, and I went on a few long drives. Eventually, I decided to meet this mysterious *Jill*.

I told my parents what my plans were, and my mom took it hard. She still isn't 100 percent okay with everything, but she's supportive and our relationship is stronger than ever. Shortly after talking with my parents, I found Jill's name on Facebook and sent her a message. I can't remember the contents of what I wrote, but I can remember being very cautious. We talked via Facebook for a week or so, and I felt comfortable enough to meet her at a coffee shop a few minutes from both of our houses.

It was definitely strange at first. I look a lot like my dad, and since I didn't have any frame of reference for Jill, I was shocked at how much I actually did look like her, as well. We spent a couple of hours asking and answering questions and giving the highlights of our lives.

Five years later, I am the recipient of silly videos sent from her daughters via Jill's phone, her husband's steak-night partner and fellow model building enthusiast, as well as a part of Jill's day-to-day life. She has always been respectful of the boundaries I've wanted to keep, and I can't thank her enough for that. I've become a permanent part of the Murphy family, and while I don't visit as often as I should, I know I am always welcome.

From Mike Murphy

"**ADOPT? FROM A** *FOREIGN* country? Are you kidding me? How am I going to be able love someone *else's* children, much less children who are completely different than me?" Those were the thoughts that raced through my head after Jill and I received the news that biological children were just not meant to be for us.

Now, before you judge me, a little background information is in order. I grew up in "white-bread America farm country"—southern Minnesota. *Everyone* looked like me. "Other kinds" of people appeared on the nightly news and were from faraway places like Minneapolis! My first taste of diversity came at age thirteen in the mid-1970s. After the Vietnam War ended, hundreds of refugees from Laos and Cambodia streamed into our "neck of the woods." Then, at the age of eighteen, I moved to the Twin Cities to take a course in radio broadcasting. Talk about culture shock! My world was changing rapidly.

As a young man, I had a very different view of the family structure. My parents divorced when I was nine, and my mom was "burdened" with raising three kids on a meager salary. She did a very good job, and we never lacked for anything. I was astounded at her ability to pull it off—"robbing Peter to pay Paul" month after month. She is an amazing person, and I will be forever grateful for all she has taught me.

Although my father is a big part of my life now, our relationship took many years to develop. After the split, Dad was someone I only saw occasionally—mostly at holidays or on birthdays. I didn't really understand why we couldn't have a normal family—with a mom *and* a dad under the same roof, like everyone else. I knew something was out of place, but only much later in life would I realize what was missing.

As I "matured" I began to enjoy my freedom. Doing what I wanted, when I wanted—with no strings attached. This way of living was new and exciting! It was also very dangerous. The highway of my life became littered with broken dreams and failed relationships. It seemed I was looking for love and validation in all the wrong places. I felt like a child in a man's body—navigating an unfriendly and very unforgiving world.

Things began to turn around for me in 1992. I learned how to sell advertising and began to earn a decent wage for the first time in my life. Then, God gave me favor by allowing me to meet the girl of my dreams! I had taken my dad's place in the Murphy Brothers Band and we were the entertainment at a wedding in my hometown. From the moment I saw Jill, there was no doubt in my mind that she was the one for me. (The fact that she did the alligator in a bridesmaid dress didn't hurt either!) Two years later, we were married.

Honestly, the thought of having children scared me to death. First of all, I thought of myself as a selfish man with a lot of hobbies and interests, not to mention a demanding job. Where would I find the time to do all the things I wanted and needed to do once the little ones arrived? Secondly, I saw my friends as they began to move into the family lifestyle. They changed! There were no more happy hours at a moment's notice or partying until 3:00 a.m. for them. It was daycare and dirty diapers, which seemed completely dull! Their lives were over—at least until the kids left for college. And then there was my perception of family. Kids seemed to be a liability—making once-great relationships turn sour with the added responsibilities and pressures.

As we learned that biological children would not be part of the plan, I breathed a sigh of relief. I dodged the bullet! God knew I was unfit to be a parent. This was all part of His plan to keep me comfortable in the lifestyle I had grown accustomed to living. Thank you, Lord.

Then Jill said, "Let's adopt."

My response was to swallow hard and mutter, "Adopt? You mean like get another cat, right? Sure. We'll just have to buy that new multi-cat litter, but…"

Jill followed with, "Let's adopt from another country. Did you know they are only allowed to have one child per family in China?"

In the back of my mind I was still thinking zero was a good number. Besides, adopt…from a *foreign* country? Are you kidding me?

Then she finally got to me and that was it—my resistance was dissolved. We were going on a journey to adoption. We eventually "acquired" two beautiful little bundles of joy from Korea: Maddie in 2001 and Olivia in 2004. Besides meeting Jesus and Jill, my girls are the very best that this life could ever offer me. "I'm a dad!" The thought still blows me away. I can't wait to see them every day, and I can't imagine my life without them.

Then, in 2010, I acquired a son! Jill had placed Joshua for adoption when she was a teen. Through God's mercy and providence, they were reunited, and he has become a beloved part of our family.

Would I be able to love my adopted children? What a silly question. The answer, of course, is a definitive "yes!"

In the end, we're all adopted. Galatians 4:3–5 expresses it best: "Even so we, when we were children, were in bondage under the elements of the world. But when the fullness of the time had come, God sent forth His Son, born of a woman, born under the law, to redeem those who were under the law, that we might receive the adoption as sons."

Interview with My Daughters, Maddie (14) and Olivia (12)

When is the first time you realized you didn't look like me or Dad?

Maddie: *Not sure how old I was. I just knew my eyes were different.*

Olivia: *Around 6…I thought, "If I have these type of eyes, how come my parents don't?"*

When you hear the word adopted, what does it mean to you?

Maddie: *It means I came to be with my loving family.*

Olivia: *Lucky!*

What feelings do you have about your birth mother?

Maddie: *I wonder if she is nice and beautiful.*

Olivia: *I'm not sure. I wonder what she looks like. I wonder if she has other kids. I know she thinks about me.*

How did you feel when you first learned about Joshua?

Maddie: *AWESOME because I never knew I had a brother.*

Olivia: *I was a little confused, but wanted to meet him.*

How do you feel about him now that he is part of our family?

Maddie: *AWESOME even though he picks on me! (chuckle)*

Olivia: *He is pretty cool and funny. I am happy he is part of it!*

When people ask you about being adopted, what do you say?

Maddie: *Well, it was a pretty good experience because I found my forever family.*

Olivia: *No one really asks. But when they do, I tell them that my birth mom was too young to be a good mom so she put me up for adoption. Then my parents wanted another daughter at the same time and they adopted me. Now I am here!*

If you had to come up with one word to describe being adopted, what word would you use?

Maddie: *Loved.*

Olivia: *Fortunate.*

Would you like to meet your birth mother someday?

Maddie: *Not sure.*

Olivia: *Yes.*

If you could say anything to your birth mother, what would it be?

Maddie: *I love you. Thanks for giving birth to me. Thanks for putting me up for adoption.*

Olivia: *Who is my birth dad? Thank you for choosing adoption for me. How old are you?*

If you could say one thing to Dad and me, what would it be?

Maddie: *Why do you love me so much?*

Olivia: *Thanks for adopting me!*

THE LETTERS

To all couples struggling with infertility,

I know this is a hard thing to go through. It's something you want so badly and just…can't…reach…it. It can be frustrating and devastating, all wrapped into one big struggle. It's not fun taking the most intimate part of your relationship and turning it into a science experiment month after month. Not only are you stressed out, anxious, hurt, and at times mad, but now the fun part of your relationship has turned all clinical.

It is one of the hardest things couples will go through. It will test your marriage and your faith. You will be angry every time someone else announces their pregnancy, when deep down you want to be happy for them. All the feelings you are having are normal. There will be times when you want to tell people to shut up and mind their own business—that is okay.

Make sure you have a doctor who understands you, is patient with you, and can even break the tension with a lighthearted joke. Sometimes we forget to laugh and have a moment during the struggle. Take time for one another as a couple that doesn't have anything to do with family talk. It is so easy to get caught up in the emotion, timing, and technicality of it all that we forget who we are individually and as a couple. You need to come up for air and breathe.

The pain you go through month after month, test after test, and even year after year is indescribable at times. It is always nice when you find another couple or person who has gone through what you are going through. It's like FINALLY someone really understands the agony.

Don't give up on your dream!!! You might end up with a beautiful family in a whole different way. Trust the journey, trust your heart. Know when to say enough is enough and try plan B. That is not giving up, that is "rerouting" your journey to becoming parents. Sometimes the feeling of closing one door and opening another can feel like a large weight has been lifted from your shoulders.

SIDE NOTE: This is a little Public Service Announcement: I am also guilty of this as well, but I want everyone reading this to take note and to spread the word…Another couple's family planning is not your business. I know the question, "So, when are you two having kids?" seems innocent enough to ask, but stop and think and wait for them to offer any info. This may be a couple that doesn't want to have children, that has been struggling to get pregnant, or that may have even lost a baby through miscarriage. You simply don't know and to be frank, it is none of your concern. Every time a couple is asked that question, it is a big slap-in-the-face reminder of the struggle they are having. It rips off a Band- Aid that they may have just put on. Be sensitive. You simply don't know someone else's struggle. Advice doesn't help either. All we hear is "blah blah blah." When what we want is a simple, "I'm here if you need anything." It is that simple.

Couples, cling to one another. You will get through this one way or another. Let go and trust. There ARE people out there who understand your journey.

Keep your faith. You are loved and understood. You will be great parents!

To all birth moms,

Whether you are a pregnant teen or young woman not ready to be a mother, I understand. This is a bump in your road you never imagined or planned at this point in your life. Right now you are feeling scared, unsure of what to do or where to go. Everything you are feeling is normal and perfectly okay. Take a deep breath and know things will be okay. You need to find someone you trust and can find support in. This could be the father of the baby, your parents, a relative, or a person you look up to. Talk to this person. I was scared to death to have my parents know. But they ended up being my greatest support. If that isn't the case for you—find someone else. You could even call me! Get all the information you need on the many decisions you have to choose from. YOU have choices! You don't need to rush into a decision. No one can make this decision for you.

Today there are so many agencies and places that are there to help you. You are lucky in this day and age. You do not have to hide and be ashamed. You aren't whisked away to some home for unwed mothers and told to never speak of this again. If you choose to keep your baby or make an adoption plan, there are places you can go for support. The one thing I cannot stress enough—*make the best choice for the baby*. It is hard to put a baby's needs before your own wants and needs. Trust me, I know.

There were two women a world away who were faced with the same decisions I was faced with. They happened to choose adoption. Because of their choice my husband and I have two beautiful daughters. The choice they made to give a part of their heart away filled the void in our hearts that we couldn't have our own children. There are not enough "thank you's" in the world for that sacrifice. They chose what was right for their babies and their selves. I am sure there is not a day that goes by that they don't think about their babies, wonder about their babies, and have an ache in their heart for their babies. I had all those feelings when I chose adoption for my son. It never goes away, but you find peace in the fact that your baby has a warm and loving home and is loved.

In our home we talk about my daughter's birth moms openly. Someday we will make that journey if they want to find them. I feel fortunate being on both sides of the adoption coin. I KNOW how their birth moms felt and that they DO think about them every day. I look forward to the day they want to find and possibly meet them. I want to be right there with them to thank those girls who are now women. I think of those women every year on Mother's Day and say a little prayer for them.

When you choose adoption you are not "giving away," "giving up," or "not keeping" your baby. You are consciously making the choice to have an adoption plan. It is one of the most selfless things a person can do. You are actually loving a baby enough to give it more that you can. It doesn't make you less of a mom. It makes you a special mom—a mom who created and gave life to this little person. You will always be a part of each other.

A piece of advice…Never be too proud to talk to someone about your feelings and emotions. I didn't and it took me twenty-plus years until I dealt with it. While I know my decision was right, I didn't process it properly. I didn't realize I was kind of a wreck about it until later in life.

Never feel ashamed. Never feel alone. There is someone who knows what you are going through and does understand. You just need to find that person or group. Once you do—it is like a weight is lifted because others "get it."

You are loved and appreciated. You are beautiful and strong.

To my daughters and any adopted child,

First thing I want you to know is that you are loved. In fact you are loved by more people than you think. You are lucky enough to have two mothers who love you. One is the woman who loved you enough to bring you into this world and loved you enough to give you a better life than what she could. The other is the woman who you call *Mom*. This woman raised you—cared for you—got to experience all the milestones with you.

Your birth mother is a woman who cared more about the well-being of YOU and put your needs before her own. She didn't just "give you away"—she consciously made the decision for you to have a better life. Whatever the circumstances were behind her choice, it was made out of love. I am sure there isn't a day that goes by that she doesn't think about you, wonder about you, and hope that you are well. Every year on your birthday she thinks of you, maybe says a prayer, and possibly sheds some tears. It's an emotional day that birth moms aren't quite sure how to feel about. Should they feel grief? Happiness? Love? Or perhaps all the above?

You may be a teen, young woman, or even a mother yourself. Whether you have met your birth mom, had communication with her or not...she DOES think and wonder about you. Birth moms want the absolute best for their child. I have spoken with quite a few birth moms in all scenarios. They all have said similar things: "I just want to know that he (or she) is okay and happy."

One thing I do want to say: if you ever want to find your birth family—it is your right and it is a natural feeling. I believe you need to find the missing piece of your own puzzle. It doesn't mean you love your family any less. You just might need closure. That is okay. As an adoptive mom I am sure my daughters will someday want to find out more about their birth moms. If they do I will be there and help in any way. I know that I am their mom and they are my daughters. I am secure in that relationship we have. Why wouldn't they be curious? Besides, I would love to meet the woman who made me a mom.

I know not every situation is sunshine and rainbows, but the fact that you have people who gave you life and people who made you their life, is beautiful. Not everyone wants a reunion. That is okay too. I see people who wait too long and have the "Should haves, would haves, could haves" or "If my birth mom wanted to know me she would have been in contact." Let me tell you, your birth mom might think the same thing. If it is something you want—there are ways to pursue it. You are not disgracing your current family by wanting to connect with your past. There is no "playbook" for this. You follow your heart.

Please remember you are loved. You are thought of. You are cherished.

Dear Jill,

As I sit here and read over your story, I realize just how much we have been through. Being seventeen, pregnant, and so scared. Scared to tell anyone…scared to accept the truth of it all…scared of what all those other people would think. How glad we were to not be in our small town in New York anymore, but away at school with crowds of unknown people. People who wouldn't judge or spread the shock and awe of the situation.

Remember how alone we felt? How we thought our parents would kick us out, disown us, and be mortified that their daughter *had sex AND got pregnant??!!!* How surprised we were at their support and unconditional love, and how they hid their anxiety, shame, and disappointment over it all so they could be there for us? I think back at how they put forth so much positivity just to help us get through it all. How they couldn't wait for the baby to be born, to move forward and pick up life where it had left off the day they'd learned of the pregnancy.

Joshua ended up being raised by his father and the woman who became his "forever" mom. It wasn't the plan we had. We were so angry and sad that our plans were surprisingly changed. But we moved on, forgave, and accepted. The best part of it all…Joshua ended up in a great family with a mother and father to love him. He got everything we wanted for him after all. My heart feels full for both us!

One thing I will always regret is that we never fully felt and dealt with the emotions of it all.

Mike came into our lives and our hearts were full, happy, and so in love. We wed and so wanted a family. The laughs, tears, and heartache of trying to start one was an experience that changed the way we felt about life's miracles, God, and all that creating a life entails. We went through all the heartbreak of not being able to conceive and came out on the other side of it stronger and more determined.

South Korea—who knew?!! The only knowledge of Korea we had was watching old 8mm movies of Dad in the service. But now we have a knowledge of the culture and can say a few words in Korean. The best part of South Korea is Madeline and Olivia. How blessed to have two beautiful daughters and now a family! The family we always wanted!

Meeting Joshua, I think we can agree, was the diamond in the rough. Finally the timing was right; God's plan was all coming together. We finally understood that God's plan was the one we needed to trust no matter how painful parts could be. Finding Joshua and now having him in our life is a true blessing and a gift we will never take for granted.

Those feelings we packed away twenty-plus years ago have come out. We have unfolded them, worked the wrinkles out, and now know that the way we feel is real and it is *okay*. It's okay to still have feelings of sadness, confusion, and hurt along with happiness, clarity, and peace. We will still have our days of tears and find it hard to process certain things…but damn it, girl, we survived! Look how beautiful life is now, once the clouds have cleared?

I wish I could have had a crystal ball back then to show you how it would all work out and we would be sitting here writing a book about this amazing journey. But you needed to go through all the ups and downs, laughter and heartache for us to truly meet and become one in peace. I believe we have begun to heal what was hurting. We have become one again and can use our story to help others who still need to begin their healing and feel complete.

Much Love,
Your older, wiser self

The home I grew up in—Chadwicks, New York. I have so many fond memories growing up there. It is the place where I really learned what a family looked like.

May 1966: My parents' wedding. This May will be fifty years! They have taught me so much about relationships, family, and being a parent.

January 1971: I was three in this picture, weeks before my
sister was born.

1977: Holly, Robert, and I. I guess my sister missed out on
the train denim outfit memo. She has always been the better
dresser!

1993: My family. We all have better hair and style now!

September 2015: Mike and I married twenty-one years. I love
this man more than words!

May 2010: The day in the coffee shop when I first met
Joshua.

August 2015: Olivia, me, and Maddie—These two make me
laugh (and pull my hair out) every day! I can't imagine life
without them.

October 2015: Joshua, Mike, Maddie, me, and Olivia. The
first time I had us all in one picture.

October 2015: These three make my heart so full with love.

2015: Me and Jennifer. She is the mutual friend of Joshua and me. We are still very close and have a fun relationship!

Summer 2014: Me, my brother Rob, and my sister Holly. For the most part, we clean up pretty well!

August 2015: Mike, me, and our beautiful daughters. Good things come to those who wait!

ACKNOWLEDGMENTS

I have so many people who helped me get this book to where it is now. To all of you, a big THANK YOU!

Mike – Thank you for being you. You helped me during this whole process both emotionally and as my personal proofreader and editor in the early stages. You have been as much a part of this journey as I have. I love our family. I love you. Xo

My parents – From the first moment you learned I was pregnant and scared at age seventeen you have been by my side with support and your unconditional love. You have been an example to me of how to be the best parent I can be. I love you both so much! We have an awesome, fun-loving family!

Holly – You are the best sister in the world!! You have always been there for me. You have helped me realize there is no "playbook" for all of this. Love you, Mr. Big, Josie, and Lili.

Robert – You were so young when this journey started for me. You probably didn't even know where babies came from! You are the best brother! Love you, KC, Coop, and baby.

Friends – You all know who you are! Some of you have been there since the very beginning. You have supported me, loved me, and made me laugh when I needed to! You all are so amazing and make my days better. Your support has really been key to this whole book process! Love you all!!

Twink – So much I could say—I love you.

Catholic Charities and Children's Home Society of MN – You helped be the bookends of becoming a mother. For every pregnant teen, infertile couple, adoptive parent, adoptee, and for your support in post-adoption situations— thank you! It is places like yours that help all of us in these life events.

Suzy and Betsy from Catholic Charities – I love our once-a-month group! How I wish I had known about you years prior. With you and our group, I have begun to heal and been able to move forward to now help others. I love all of you who come each month. Our stories are different, yet we all have a beautiful connection. To find people who truly "get it" is so comforting. The bond this group shares is priceless.

Pat and Stacy – I admire and respect you both so much. Who was to say my plan was any better way back then? You have raised an amazing son. He is lucky to have you as parents, along with a wonderful family.

Karen Z. – You put the seed in my head to do something with my story years ago. Thank you for your support, guidance, and for being a great teacher/mentor.

Jessica Freeburg – Thank you for saying "yes" and agreeing to be my cowriter on this project. You took my crazy, emotional ramblings and turned them into a story that was still mine, but read BEAUTIFULLY! Rock on, GHOSTwriter. :-)

Tera Girardin – Thanks for making me look pretty for my book! *Teraphotography.com*

Galit Breen – Thank you for reading my book and sending it on! You set me up with a wonderful team and you have been a great cheerleader! #kindnesswins

Booktrope team – Pam Labbe, Michelle Fairbanks (at Fresh Design), Andie Gibson, Tricia Parker, and Heather Huffman! You are all awesome to work with!! Everyone else at Booktrope—thank you!

A big THANK YOU to all of you who have followed me, shared me, and liked me on social media through this process. Keep on sharing!!

ABOUT THE AUTHOR

Jill M. Murphy is an author, a blogger, an assistant preschool teacher, a wife, and a mother. In her free time you might find her taking a discarded chair or table off the side of the road to repurpose it into something new and fun. She also loves to read, cook, entertain, and laugh. Murphy lives outside of St. Paul, Minnesota, with her husband and two daughters.

Be sure to check out Jill's website and blog:

www.jillmmurphy.com
www.jillsy.wordpress.com

And connect on social media:

Twitter:
@Jillsymurph

Facebook:

www.facebook.com/FindingMotherhood

Made in the USA
Middletown, DE
29 March 2019